1,000
Q&A

First published by Parragon in 2013

Parragon
Chartist House
15–17 Trim Street
Bath BA1 1HA, UK
www.parragon.com

ISBN 978-1-4723-1151-1

Printed in China

Parragon

Bath • New York • Singapore • Hong Kong • Cologne • Delhi
Melbourne • Amsterdam • Johannesburg • Shenzhen

CONTENTS

WHAT IS...

A solar system is made up of a star and all the objects orbiting or circling it. Our solar system includes the Sun, eight planets and their moons, and other balls of rock, ice and metal, such as comets and asteroids. The Sun makes up 99% of the solar system's mass.

A SOLAR SYSTEM?

The solar system began as a cloud of gas and dust and slowly took shape over billions of years. While the Sun is at the centre of our solar system, the Sun itself is orbiting the centre of our galaxy, the Milky Way. It takes our solar system about 225 to 250 million years to complete one orbit of the Milky Way.

HOW OLD IS...

...THE SUN?

The Sun is a middle-aged star. It probably formed about 4.6 billion years ago. It will probably burn for another 5 billion years and then die in a blaze so bright that the Earth will be scorched right out of existence.

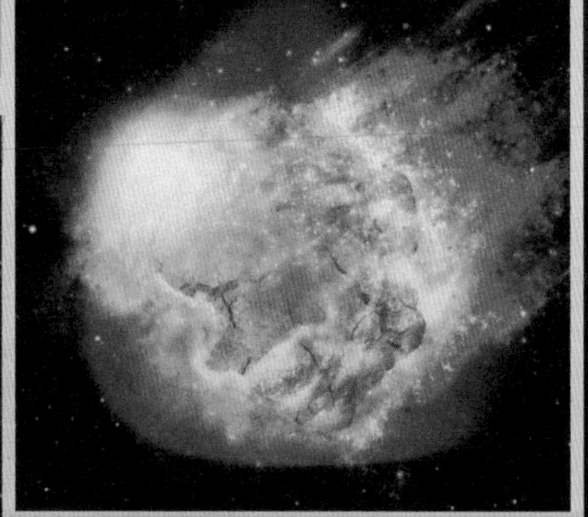

... THE EARTH?

The Earth was born about 4.6 billion years ago.

... THE UNIVERSE?

Scientists believe that the Universe may be 13.7 billion years old.

HOW LONG IS...

... A YEAR?

The Earth travels around the Sun every 365.24 days, which gives us our calendar year of 365 days. To make up the extra 0.24 days, we add an extra day to our calendar at the end of February in every fourth year, known as a leap year.

... A YEAR ON MERCURY?

It takes approximately 88 Earth days for Mercury to travel around the Sun – so a year on Mercury is about a quarter of an Earth year.

... A YEAR ON NEPTUNE?

Neptune is so far from the Sun that its orbit takes about 165 Earth years. So one year on Neptune lasts for 165 Earth years.

... A MONTH?

A lunar month is 29.53 days long. It takes the Moon 27.3 days to circle the Earth, but it is 29.53 days from one full moon to the next, because the Earth is also moving. Our calendar months are artificial.

... A DAY?

A day is the time the Earth takes to turn once. Our day (the solar day) is 24 hours.

HOW BIG IS...

	Diameter in kilometres	Surface area (million sq km)
...THE SUN?	1,391,000	6,078,747
... MERCURY?	4,880	75
...VENUS?	12,104	460
...THE EARTH?	12,757	510
... MARS?	6,794	144
... JUPITER?	142,984	61,418
... SATURN?	120,536	42,612
... URANUS?	51,118	8,083
... NEPTUNE?	49,528	7,618
...THE MOON?	3,475	38

HOW BIG IS THE SUN?

Compared to the Earth the Sun is massive, but compared to other stars it's only small to medium-sized.

HOW BIG IS JUPITER?

Very big! Even though Jupiter is largely gas, it weighs 318 times as much as the Earth.

HOW BIG IS THE EARTH?

Satellite measurements show it is 40,030 kilometres around the equator.

HOW DID...

Around 4.6 billion years ago, a cloud of gas and dust swirled around our newly formed Sun. Gradually, the grains of dust and gas were pulled together into clumps by their own gravity. These clumps became the Earth and the other planets in our solar system.

WHAT WAS THE EARLY EARTH LIKE?

It was a fiery ball. It took half a billion years for its surface to cool and form a hard crust. As it cooled, the Earth gave off gases and water vapour, which formed the atmosphere.

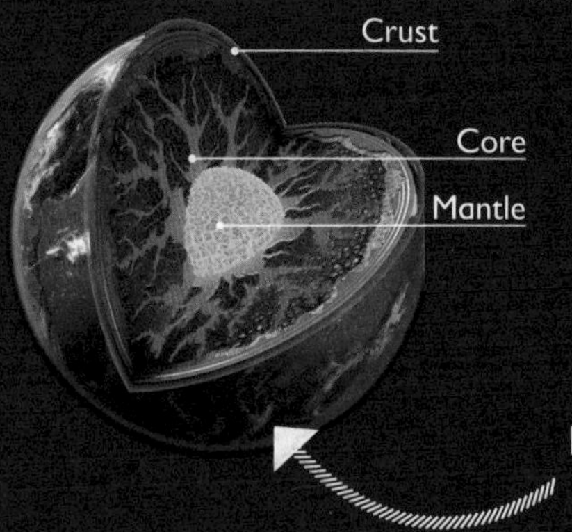

WHAT IS THE EARTH MADE OF?

Its core consists mainly of iron. Its rocky crust is made mostly of oxygen and silicon. In between the two layers is the hot mantle of metal silicates, sulphides and oxides.

WHAT'S SPECIAL ABOUT THE EARTH?

The Earth is the only planet with oxygen in its atmosphere and liquid water on its surface. Both water and oxygen are needed for life to exist.

WHAT IS THE ATMOSPHERE?

The Earth's atmosphere, or 'air', is a layer of gases – including nitrogen, oxygen, argon and carbon dioxide – that surrounds the planet.

THE EARTH BEGIN?

DOES THE EARTH SPIN?

The Earth spins on its axis once a day, while also orbiting, or travelling around, the Sun.

WHAT SHAPE IS THE EARTH?

The Earth is not quite a perfect sphere. The spinning of the planet causes it to bulge at the equator. Scientists describe Earth's shape as 'geoid', which simply means Earth-shaped!

HOW OLD ARE OCEANS?

The oceans were formed between 3.8 and 4.2 billion years ago. As the Earth cooled, clouds of steam became water, creating vast oceans.

WHAT ARE TIDES?

Tides are caused by the oceans being pulled by the Moon's gravity. On the side of the Earth facing the Moon, the oceans are pulled more than the Earth. On the opposite side, the water is pulled less than the Earth itself.

HOW OLD IS EARTH'S OLDEST ROCK?

Earth's oldest rock is 4.28 billion years old.

WHAT IS A GAS GIANT?

Jupiter, Saturn, Uranus and Neptune are all gas giants. This means that they are large planets made mostly from gases such as hydrogen and helium. They do not have a solid surface because they are not made of rock or other hard minerals.

WHAT IS A DWARF PLANET?

There are five dwarf planets currently known in the solar system: Pluto, Ceres, Makemake, Eris and Haumea. These are large enough to be rounded by their own gravity but not large enough to have cleared the area around them. Pluto was called a planet until 2006, when it was reclassified.

WHAT ARE THE ICE GIANTS?

Neptune and Uranus are sometimes known as ice giants because they contain a large amount of icy water, methane and ammonia. These are the two planets farthest from the Sun.

WHAT IS...

... SUNSET? The Earth turns on its axis once every 24 hours. The Sun appears to rise in the east, moving across the sky to set in the west.

... SUMMER? As the Earth orbits the Sun, the hemisphere of the planet tilted towards the Sun has its summer.

... THE SOLAR CYCLE? The Sun follows a cycle of activity called the Solar Cycle, which lasts about 11 years.

...THE SUN?

The Sun is the star at the centre of our solar system. It was formed from a cloud of gas and dust, and material from one or more exploding stars. Light and heat from the Sun support all life on Earth.

...A SOLAR ECLIPSE? A solar eclipse is when the Moon moves in between the Sun and the Earth, creating a shadow on the Earth.

... A SUNSPOT? Sunspots are dark blotches seen on the Sun's surface. They are dark because they are slightly less hot than the rest of the surface.

...A TRANSIT? Mercury and Venus are closer to the Sun than Earth. Occasionally they can be seen crossing, or in transit over, the face of the Sun.

... THE SUN'S CROWN? The Sun's crown is its corona, its glowing white-hot atmosphere.

... THE SOLAR WIND? The solar wind is a stream of particles constantly blowing out from the Sun.

... A SOLAR FLARE? Flares are eruptions on the Sun's surface that release energy into space.

... MOONLIGHT?

Moonlight is the Sun's light reflected off the dust on the Moon's surface.

... WAXING?

Over the first two weeks of each month, we see more and more of the Moon's bright side until full moon. As the Moon appears to grow, we say that it is waxing. As the Moon appears to shrink, we say that it is waning.

... A NEW MOON?

At the new moon, the Moon lies between the Earth and the Sun, and we catch only a crescent-shaped glimpse of its bright side.

... THE MOON?

The Moon is a rocky ball and is the Earth's natural satellite. It is held in orbit around the Earth by gravity and has circled the Earth for at least 4 billion years. It is about a quarter of the Earth's diameter.

... A LUNAR ECLIPSE?

As the Moon goes around the Earth, sometimes it passes right into Earth's shadow, where sunlight is blocked off. This is a lunar eclipse.

WHO WAS...

... COPERNICUS?

Nicolaus Copernicus (1473–1543) was the Polish astronomer who first suggested the Earth was moving around the Sun. Before this, most people thought everything in the Universe revolved around the Earth.

... GALILEO GALILEI?

Saturn's rings are the planet's shining halo, first seen by Galileo Galilei, who invented a simple telescope in 1609.

... CASSINI?

In 1675, the astronomer Cassini spotted a dark gap between the rings around Saturn. This is now called the Cassini Division, after him.

... EDMUND HALLEY?

Edmund Halley (1656–1742) was the first person to correctly predict the year in which a particular comet would reappear. That comet was later named after him.

... WILLIAM HERSCHEL?

Herschel first discovered Uranus in 1781, thinking it was a comet. Uranus was soon proved to be a planet.

1400

1600

1700

... JOHN COUCH ADAMS?

John Couch Adams was a British mathematician who predicted Neptune's position at the same time as Frenchman Urbain le Verrier. Both men looked at the way Neptune's gravity disturbed Uranus' orbit.

... JOHANN GALLE?

In Berlin, Johann Galle was the first to spot Neptune, on 23 September, 1846.

... ASAPH HALL?

In 1877, American astronomer Asaph Hall discovered Mars' two moons. He named them Phobos and Deimos after the attendants of the Roman war god, Mars.

... THE FIRST DOG IN SPACE?

The first living creature in space was a dog named Laika. She was sent into orbit in 1957.

... THE FIRST PERSON TO WALK ON THE MOON?

The first men on the Moon were Neil Armstrong and Buzz Aldrin of the US Apollo 11 mission. They landed on the Moon on 20 July, 1969.

1800

1900

THE PLANETS

HOW HOT IS MERCURY?

In the day, temperatures soar to 400°C; at night they plunge to -175°C.

IS THERE LIFE ON MARS?

Images from the mountains of Mars in 2011 showed signs of flowing water, suggesting that micro-organisms may be able to survive.

HOW FAST DOES JUPITER SPIN?

Despite its huge size, Jupiter's surface moves at 45,000 kilometres an hour – faster than any other planet!

WHY IS VENUS CALLED THE EVENING STAR?

Venus reflects sunlight so well that it shines like a star. We can see it just before sunrise and also in the evening, just after the Sun sets.

HOW HEAVY IS SATURN?

Made largely of hydrogen, Saturn is remarkably light, with a mass of 600 billion trillion tonnes. If you could find a big enough bath to put it in, it would float.

HOW WINDY IS NEPTUNE?

Neptune's winds roar around the planet at up to 2,100 kilometres an hour!

WHAT'S STRANGE ABOUT URANUS?

Unlike any of the other planets, Uranus does not spin on a slight tilt. Instead it is tilted right over and rolls around the Sun on its side, like a giant bowling ball.

WHAT COLOUR IS NEPTUNE?

The methane gas in Neptune's atmosphere absorbs red light, making the planet appear greeny-blue.

WHAT IS JUPITER'S RED SPOT?

The Great Red Spot or GRS is a huge swirling storm in Jupiter's atmosphere.

WHY IS MARS RED?

Mars is red because the surface contains iron dust. Small amounts of oxygen in the atmosphere turn this rusty.

The planets are not alone out there. Balls of ice, rock and metal also circle and hurtle through the solar system. But what exactly are they?

WHAT IS...

... AN ASTEROID?	Asteroids are mostly made of rock and metal. Thousands of asteroids circle round the Sun in a big band between Mars and Jupiter.
... A COMET?	Comets are balls of dirty ice in the outer solar system. Occasionally, one is drawn towards the Sun. Material from its surface is blown away, making a shining tail.
... A METEORITE?	Meteorites are lumps of rock from space that are big enough to penetrate the Earth's atmosphere and reach the ground without burning up.
... THE KUIPER BELT?	It is a region of the solar system that lies beyond Neptune. Thousands of relatively small, frozen objects orbit there.
... A RING SYSTEM?	The gas giants have ring systems containing billions of chips of ice and dust that circle each planet like a halo.

WHAT IS...

A galaxy is a massive system of stars, gas and dust, held together by gravity. There are billions of galaxies scattered throughout space. Sometimes they merge or collide with each other.

A GALAXY?

Our galaxy is called the Milky Way. This is because it can be seen stretching across the night sky in a blotchy white band. This is our edge-on view of the galaxy. Since our own galaxy was the first one that astronomers knew about, they came up with the word 'galaxy', which comes from the Greek word for milky.

WHAT IS THE UNIVERSE?

Scientists define the Universe as absolutely everything that physically exists. It is believed that the Universe was created by the Big Bang.

WHAT WAS THERE BEFORE THE UNIVERSE?

No one knows. Some people think there was a vast ocean, beyond space and time, of potential universes continually bursting into life or failing.

WHAT WAS THE BIG BANG?

In the beginning, all the Universe was squeezed into a tiny, hot, dense ball. The Big Bang was when this suddenly began to swell explosively, allowing energy and matter, then atoms, gas clouds and galaxies to form.

THE BIG BANG!

WHAT IS GRAVITY?

Gravity is the invisible force of attraction between every bit of matter in the Universe, such as between the Earth and the Sun.

WHAT IS THE UNIVERSE MADE FROM?

The stars and clouds in space are made almost 100% of hydrogen and helium. Rocky planets formed from concentrations of elements such as carbon, oxygen, silicon, nitrogen and iron.

HOW HOT WAS THE BIG BANG?

As the Universe grew from smaller than an atom to the size of a football, it cooled from infinity to ten billion billion billion°C.

WHAT WAS THE UNIVERSE LIKE AT THE BEGINNING?

The early Universe was very small, but contained all the matter and energy in the Universe today. It lasted only a split second.

HOW DO WE KNOW WHAT THE EARLY UNIVERSE WAS LIKE?

Machines called colliders and particle accelerators can recreate conditions in the early Universe by using magnets to accelerate particles and crash them together.

WHAT IS INFLATION?

Inflation was when dramatic expansion and cooling took place just a tiny fraction of a second after the Big Bang.

HOW DID THE FIRST GALAXIES FORM?

They formed from lumps of clouds of hydrogen and helium, as concentrations within the clumps drew together.

WHAT ARE IRREGULAR GALAXIES?

Irregular galaxies are galaxies that have no particular shape at all.

WHAT ARE SPIRAL GALAXIES?

Spiral galaxies are spinning Catherine wheel spirals like our Milky Way.

HOW MANY GALAXIES ARE THERE?

There are currently estimated to be about 125 billion galaxies in the Universe.

ARE GALAXIES IN GROUPS?

Yes. Most galaxies are in clusters, which can form larger groups called superclusters.

WHAT ARE ELLIPTICAL GALAXIES?

Elliptical galaxies are shaped like rugby balls. There is no gas and dust remaining in an elliptical galaxy, so no new stars can form.

WHAT IS...

... A NUCLEUS?

The nucleus, or centre, of an atom is made of protons and neutrons, which are themselves made of quarks.

... AN ATOM?

Atoms are the smallest bit of any substance. Atoms are made up of empty space and even tinier particles.

... ANTI-MATTER?

Anti-matter is the mirror image of ordinary matter. If matter and anti-matter meet, they destroy each other. Fortunately, there is no anti-matter on Earth.

... AN ATOM SMASHER?

An atom smasher is used to propel particles at extremely high speeds so that we can find out more about them.

... A QUARK?

A quark is one of the smallest particles inside the nucleus. Quarks were among the first particles to form at the birth of the Universe.

... MATTER?

Matter is simply anything that has mass and takes up space. All matter is made up of tiny particles, such as protons, neutrons and electrons. Particles are the building blocks of the Universe.

HOW SMALL IS A QUARK?

It is less than 10^{-20} metres across, which means a line of ten billion billion of them would be less than a metre long.

HOW WERE ATOMS MADE?

Atoms of hydrogen and helium were made in the early days of the Universe when quarks joined together. All other atoms were made as atoms were fused together by the intense heat and pressure inside stars.

HOW CAN WE SEE QUARKS?

The paths of tiny particles, such as quarks, can be seen after crashing atoms together at great speed.

WHAT ARE PARTICLES?

Particles are the basic units of matter that make up everyday objects. There are hundreds of kinds of particles, but all apart from the atom and molecule are too small to see, even with the most powerful microscope.

WHAT IS...

A black hole is an area that has such a strong pull of gravity that it sucks space into a 'hole' like a funnel. Not even light can escape the pull of a black hole, which is why it is called 'black'. The hole's interior cannot be seen.

WHAT HAPPENS INSIDE A BLACK HOLE?

Nothing that goes into a black hole comes out. Everything is torn apart by the immense gravity.

HOW IS A BLACK HOLE FORMED?

When a large star explodes, the centre of the star is violently compressed by the shock of the explosion. As it compresses, it becomes denser and denser and its gravity becomes more and more powerful – until it shrinks to a single tiny point of infinite density called a singularity. The singularity sucks space into a black hole.

A BLACK HOLE?

HOW CAN WE SEE A BLACK HOLE?

The black hole contains so much matter in such a small space that its gravitational pull even drags in light. We may be able to spot a black hole from the powerful radiation emitted by stars being ripped to shreds as they are sucked in. A giant black hole may exist at the centre of our galaxy.

HOW MANY BLACK HOLES ARE THERE?

No one really knows. Because they trap light, they are hard to see. But there may be as many as **100 million** black holes in the Milky Way.

WHAT ARE...

... STARS?

Stars are gigantic glowing balls of gas, scattered throughout space. They burn for anything from a few million to tens of billions of years.

... RED GIANTS?

Red giants are huge cool stars, formed when surface gas on a medium-sized star near the end of its life swells up.

... RED DWARFS?

Red dwarfs are small and fairly cool stars with a mass of less than 40% of that of the Sun. The majority of stars are believed to be red dwarfs.

... WHITE DWARFS?

White dwarfs are the small dense stars formed when the outer layers of a star like the Sun are blown off during the last parts of the red giant stage.

... PULSARS?

Pulsars are stars that flash out intense radio pulses every ten seconds or less as they spin rapidly.

... CONSTELLATIONS?

Constellations are small patterns of stars in the sky, each with its own name.

... CLUSTERS?

Stars are rarely entirely alone within a galaxy. Many are concentrated in groups called clusters.

... DOUBLE STARS?

Our Sun is alone in space, but many stars have one or more nearby companions. Double stars are called binaries.

... THE PLEIADES?
They are a group of over 400 stars that formed in the same cloud of dust and gas.

WHERE ARE STARS BORN?

Stretched throughout space are vast clouds of dust and gas called nebulae. Stars are born in the biggest of these nebulae, which are called giant molecular clouds.

HOW ARE STARS BORN?

Stars are born when clumps of gas in space are drawn together by their own gravity, and the middle of the clump is squeezed so hard that temperatures trigger a nuclear fusion reaction. The heat makes the star shine.

WHICH IS THE NEAREST STAR? The nearest star, apart from the Sun, is Proxima Centauri. It is 40 trillion kilometres away.

WHICH ARE THE BIGGEST STARS? The biggest stars are known as supergiants. Antares is 700 times as big as the Sun.

WHAT IS A SUPERNOVA?

A supernova is a gigantic explosion. It finishes off a supergiant star. For a few minutes, the supernova flashes out with the brilliance of billions of Suns.

WHAT ARE STANDARD CANDLES? When measuring the distance to middle-distance stars, astronomers compare the star's brightness to stars that they know, or 'standard candles'.

A SUPERNOVA

THE BIRTH OF A STAR

HOW MANY STARS ARE THERE?

Astronomers guess there are about **200 billion billion** stars in the Universe. But it is hard to know – most stars are too far away to see.

HOW OLD ARE STARS?

Stars are dying and being born all the time. Big, bright stars live for only 10 million years. Medium-sized stars like our Sun live for 10 billion years.

HOW HOT IS A STAR?

The surface temperature of the coolest stars is below 3,500°C; that of the hottest, brightest stars is over 40,000°C.

HOW DOES A STAR BURN?

In medium-sized stars, the heat generated in the core pushes gas out as hard as gravity pulls it in, so the star burns steadily for billions of years.

HOW DO STARS GLOW?

Pressure deep inside each star generates nuclear fusion reactions. Hydrogen atoms fuse together, releasing huge quantities of energy.

WHAT HAPPENS WHEN STARS DIE?

When a star has used up all its energy, it either blows up, shrinks, goes cold or becomes a black hole.

WHAT IS THE HUNTER?

The constellation of Orion looks like a hunter holding a sword. The hunter's head, shoulders, three-starred belt, legs and sword can be seen.

WHICH STARS LIVE LONGEST?

The biggest stars have lots of nuclear fuel, but live fast and die young. The smallest stars have little nuclear fuel, but live slow and long.

WHY DO STARS TWINKLE?

Stars twinkle because the Earth's atmosphere is never still and starlight twinkles as the air wavers.

WHAT COLOURS ARE STARS?

The colour of medium-sized stars is shown on a graph called the main sequence. Hot stars are bright blue-white. Cool stars are dim and red.

HOW DO WE KNOW THE UNIVERSE IS GETTING BIGGER?

We can tell the Universe is getting bigger because distant galaxies are speeding away from us. The galaxies themselves are not moving – the space in between them is stretching.

HOW LONG WILL THE UNIVERSE LAST?

It depends how much matter it contains. If there is more than the 'critical density', it may begin to contract and end in a 'Big Crunch'. If there is much less, it may go on expanding forever.

HOW DID LIFE BEGIN?

Lightning flashes may have created amino acids, the basic chemicals of life, from the waters and gases of the early Earth. But no one knows how these chemicals were able to make copies of themselves.

WHAT SHAPE IS THE UNIVERSE?

Scientists do not yet know. Perhaps the Universe is flat, perhaps it is a curve or perhaps even a sphere.

WHERE IS THE EARTH?

The Earth is just over halfway out along one of the spiral arms of the Milky Way Galaxy, about 30,000 light years from the centre.

WHERE IS ANDROMEDA?

The Andromeda Galaxy is the closest large galaxy to the Milky Way.

WHAT IS LIFE MADE OF?

Life is based on compounds of the element carbon, known as organic chemicals. Carbon compounds called amino acids link up to form proteins, and proteins form the chemicals that build living cells.

WHERE DID THE MATERIALS OF LIFE COME FROM?

It used to be thought that organic chemicals all originated on Earth, but many complicated compounds have been found in molecular clouds.

HOW DO WE LOOK FOR EXTRATERRESTRIAL LIFE?

Since possible fossils of microscopic life were seen in a Martian meteorite found on Earth in 1996, scientists have hunted for other signs of organisms in rocks from space.

IS THERE LIFE ON OTHER PLANETS?

In such a large Universe there are probably many planets, like Earth, suitable for life. No one knows if life arose on Earth by a unique chance or whether it is fairly likely to happen if the conditions are right.

WHAT IS...

...THE BIGGEST THING IN THE UNIVERSE?

The biggest structure in the Universe is the Sloan Great Wall – a great sheet of galaxies that measures over a billion light years across.

...THE FARTHEST OBJECT WE CAN SEE?

The farthest object visible with the naked eye is the Andromeda Galaxy, which is about 2.5 million light years away. It is visible as a smudge in the night sky.

... A LIGHT YEAR?

A light year is 9,460,000,000,000 kilometres. This is the distance light can travel in a year, at its constant rate of 300,000 kilometres per second.

...A PARSEC?

A parsec is 3.26 light years. Parsecs are worked out geometrically from slight shifts of a star's apparent position as the Earth moves around the Sun.

... SETI?

SETI is the Search for Extra-Terrestrial Intelligence project, designed to continually scan radio signals from space and pick up any signs of intelligence.

HOW MANY...

COUNTRIES ARE THERE?

There are nearly 200 countries in the world. Some of these nations rule themselves, while some are ruled by other countries. The number of countries constantly changes as some join together to make a single nation, while others break up into smaller states.

WHO ARE THE WORLD'S PEOPLES?

Human beings who share the same history or language make up a 'people' or 'ethnic group'. Sometimes many different peoples share a country. More than 120 peoples live in Tanzania, Africa.

HOW MANY PEOPLE LIVE IN THE WORLD?

Billions! In 2012 there were about 7 billion human beings living on our planet. That's more than twice as many as 50 years ago.

7 billion humans on the planet

WHICH COUNTRY HAS THE MOST PEOPLE?

More people live in China than anywhere else in the world. They number about 1,344,000,000 and most live in the big cities of the east and the south. In the far west of China there are empty deserts and lonely mountains.

1,344,000,000

people live in China

WHAT IS...

...A CONTINENT?

The big masses of land that make up the Earth's surface are called continents. The biggest continent is Asia, home to more than 3.9 billion people.

...A COUNTRY?

A country is an area of land under the rule of a single government. Its borders have to be agreed with neighbouring countries.

... A CAPITAL CITY?

The most important city in a country is called the capital.

... A STATE?

A country is often divided into smaller regions known as states, provinces, counties or departments.

...AN EMPIRE?

An empire is a country that rules over many other countries and nations.

...A DEPENDENT NATION?

A dependent nation is ruled by another country. There are around 38 dependent nations, including many tiny islands in the Caribbean Sea and in the Atlantic and Pacific Oceans.

...AN INDEPENDENT NATION?

Independent nations rule themselves. Currently there are more than 190 independent countries in the world.

...A GOVERNMENT?

The members of the government run the country. They pass new laws on everything from schools to hospitals and businesses.

...A REPUBLIC?

It's a country that has no king or queen, such as France.

... A DEMOCRACY?

In a democracy, people vote for a political party to make the decisions.

... A PARLIAMENT?

A parliament is a meeting place where new laws are discussed and approved.

... A HEAD OF STATE?

The most important person in a country is the head of state. This may be a king or a queen or an elected president.

... THE LAW?

Laws are a system of rules that govern everything from how we elect our leaders to how we should behave towards each other.

... A NATIONAL ANTHEM?

National anthems are played or sung to show respect to a certain country. They are often played at important occasions.

... A CURRENCY?

A currency is a money system, such as the Japanese yen or the US dollar.

WHICH IS THE WORLD'S RICHEST COUNTRY?

Some economists say that Qatar, in the Middle East, is the richest country because it exports huge amounts of oil and gas.

WHICH IS THE BIGGEST COUNTRY IN THE WORLD?

The Russian Federation, measuring more than 17 million square kilometres. Its clocks are set at 9 different times!

WHICH COUNTRY HAS THREE CAPITALS?

South Africa. Cape Town is the legislative capital. Pretoria is the executive capital. Bloemfontein is the judicial capital.

WHICH IS THE OLDEST NATIONAL FLAG?

Denmark's is the oldest flag still in use. It is a white cross on a red background and was first used in the 14th century.

WHICH IS THE WORLD'S OLDEST ROYAL FAMILY?

The Japanese royal family has produced a long line of 125 reigning emperors over thousands of years.

WHICH IS THE WORLD'S OLDEST PARLIAMENT?

The oldest parliament is in Iceland. Called the Althing, it was started by Viking settlers in AD 930.

WHICH CITY IS A MEGACITY?

Tokyo is an example of a megacity, encompassing 26 other cities and 5 towns.

WHICH IS THE HIGHEST CITY?

La Rinconada in Peru is the highest city, standing at 5,100 metres above sea level.

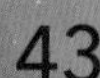

WHICH COUNTRY FITS INSIDE A CITY? The world's smallest nation is an area within the city of Rome, in Italy. It is called Vatican City and is the headquarters of the Roman Catholic Church.

WHICH CITY IS NAMED AFTER A GODDESS?
Athens, the capital of Greece, shares its name with an ancient goddess named Athena. Her beautiful temple, the Parthenon, still towers over the modern city.

HOW MANY LANGUAGES ARE THERE?

Around 6,900 languages are spoken in the world.

WHAT IS THE MOST SPOKEN LANGUAGE?

Mandarin Chinese is spoken by the most people. Around a billion people use it every day.

DOES EVERYBODY IN ONE COUNTRY SPEAK THE SAME LANGUAGE?

Not often. For example, families from all over the world have made their homes in the United States.

HOW MANY PEOPLE SPEAK ENGLISH?

English is the most widespread language: 470 million English-speakers are dotted through every single country.

WHAT IS THE LEAST SPOKEN LANGUAGE?

Fewer than 20 people in Latvia speak a language called Liv.

COULD WE INVENT ONE LANGUAGE FOR THE WHOLE WORLD?

It's already been done! A language called Esperanto was invented over 100 years ago.

CAN WE TALK WITHOUT WORDS?

People who are unable to hear or speak can use sign language to communicate.

WHAT IS BODY LANGUAGE?

Movements of the head and hands can be a kind of language. But be careful – shaking the head can mean 'yes' in some countries and 'no' in others!

DO WE ALL READ LEFT TO RIGHT?

The Arabic language is read right-to-left, and traditional Japanese top-to-bottom.

WHAT IS EMAIL?

Email, or 'electronic mail', is a way of sending and receiving messages by electronic communications systems, such as computers. The first email was sent in 1971.

HOW DO WE TALK THROUGH SPACE?

Satellites are machines sent into space to circle the Earth. They can pick up telephone, radio or television signals from one part of the world and beam them down to another.

WHAT'S IN A NAME?

In Norway there's a village called Å. In New Zealand there's a place called **Taumatawhakatangihangakoa-uauotamateapokaiwhenuakitanatahu**.

DO WE USE DIFFERENT WAYS OF WRITING?

Yes. This book is printed in the Roman alphabet, which has 26 letters and is used for many languages. Other languages use all sorts of lines and pictures.

WHAT IS THE MOST UNUSUAL WAY TO COMMUNICATE?

In some parts of Central America, Turkey and the Canary Islands, people worked out a way of communicating using whistles instead of words.

WHAT HAS MADE THE WORLD SHRINK?

The planet hasn't shrunk – it just seems that way. Today, we can send messages around the world instantly. Once, letters were sent by ship and took many months to arrive.

ARE THERE MORE AND MORE PEOPLE?

Every minute, about 260 babies are born around the world. Imagine how they would cry if they were all put together! By the year 2050 there will probably be 9.3 billion people in the world.

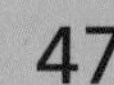

IS THERE ENOUGH ROOM FOR EVERYBODY?

Just about! But some time in the future, people may have to live in towns under the ocean or even on other planets, where they would need a special supply of air to stay alive.

WHO LIVES AT THE ENDS OF THE EARTH?

One of the world's most northerly settlements is Ny-Ålesund, in the Arctic territory of Svalbard. The southernmost city is Puerto Williams in Tierra del Fuego, Chile.

TIERRA DEL FUEGO, CHILE

HAVE HUMANS CHANGED OUR PLANET?

Over the ages, humans have changed the face of the world we live in. They have chopped down forests and dammed rivers. They have built big cities and roads.

WHY ARE SOME LANDS RICHER THAN OTHERS?

Some lands have good soil, where crops can grow. Some have oil, which is worth a lot of money. But other countries have poor soil, little rain and no minerals.

DO ALL PEOPLES HAVE A COUNTRY THEY CAN CALL THEIR OWN?

No, the ancient homelands of some peoples are divided up between other countries. The lands of the Kurdish people are split between several nations.

WHAT PROBLEMS DO CITIES CAUSE?

Too much traffic in cities often blocks up the roads and fills the air with fumes. In some cities, there isn't enough work for everyone and some people live in poor conditions.

WHAT DO BILLIONS OF PEOPLE EAT EVERY DAY?

Billions of people eat rice every day, especially in Asia. Grains of rice are the seeds of a kind of grass that grows in flooded fields called paddies.

WHO INVENTED DEMOCRACY?

The people of ancient Athens, in Greece, started the first democratic assembly nearly 2,500 years ago. It wasn't completely fair, as women and slaves weren't given the right to vote.

WHO GETS TO BECOME KING OR QUEEN?

Normally you have to be a prince or princess, born into a royal family. In the past, kings and queens were powerful. Today their role is more as the nation's figurehead, representing their country on visits and at meetings.

HOW DO YOU RECOGNIZE KINGS AND QUEENS?

For ceremonies, kings and queens wear traditional robes, and some wear crowns and carry symbols of royal power, such as golden sceptres.

WHY DO COUNTRIES HAVE FLAGS?

Flags show bold patterns and bright colours. Many flags are symbols of a nation, or of its regions. The designs on flags often tell us about a country or its history.

WHY DO WE BUILD SKYSCRAPERS?

In busy cities where land is scarce, people have to use the space above the ground, building tall skyscrapers.

WHERE...

...ARE THE BIGGEST CITIES IN THE WORLD?

In Japan. More than 36 million people live in the capital, Tokyo.

...ARE THE WORLD'S BIGGEST RANCHES?

The world's biggest sheep and cattle stations are in the Australian outback.

... IS THE BIGGEST GENERAL ELECTION?

More than 670 million people are eligible to vote in general elections in India.

... IS THE WORLD'S LONGEST ROAD?

It begins in the northern US state of Alaska and stretches right down to Central America. It is called the Pan-American Highway and covers 48,000 kilometres.

... IS THE WORLD'S BIGGEST AIRPORT?

King Fahd International Airport in Saudi Arabia covers 780 square kilometres of desert.

...WAS THE WHEEL INVENTED?

In Mesopotamia (present-day Iraq) more than 6,000 years ago.

...ARE THE LONGEST TRUCKS?

In the Australian outback, trucks can hitch on three or four giant trailers to form a 'road train' on the long, straight roads.

... IS THE MOST CROWDED PLACE IN THE WORLD?

Bangladesh is one of the most crowded places, with more than 1,000 people per square kilometre.

... WERE THE FIRST CITIES BUILT?

The first cities were built in southwest Asia. Çatal Hüyük in Turkey was begun about 9,000 years ago.

... CAN YOU CATCH A TRAIN INTO THE SKY?

In Salta, Argentina, you can catch the 'Train to the Clouds'.

... ARE BOATS USED AS BUSES?

In Venice, Italy, there are canals instead of roads. People travel by boat.

... IS THE SILK ROAD?

This is an ancient trading route stretching from China through Central Asia to the Mediterranean Sea. Silk, tea and spices were transported along this road.

... ARE THE WORLD'S BREAD BASKETS?

Important wheat-producing areas are known as 'bread baskets'. Wheat grows best in areas that were once natural grasslands, such as the American prairies.

... DO JUDGES WEAR BIG WIGS?

In Great Britain. The old-fashioned wigs are meant to show that judges stand for the law of the land.

... WERE BANKNOTES INVENTED?

Paper money was first used in China a thousand years ago.

WHAT ARE...

THE WORLD'S MAIN RELIGIONS?

The world's main religions include Islam, Hinduism, Buddhism and Judaism. The religion with the most believers – a third of the world's population – is Christianity. All faiths have their own beliefs about the nature of the world and special ways of praying and worshipping.

Most religions set down moral codes that say how believers should behave. These rules might govern how we should treat people and animals. Religious scriptures, or holy books, also tell believers how they should worship, through prayer, fasting or pilgrimage.

WHAT IS...

...THE TAO? Pronounced 'dow', it means 'the way'. It is the name given to the beliefs of the Chinese thinker Lao Zi, who lived about 2,500 years ago. Taoists believe in the harmony of the Universe.

... SHINTO? This is the ancient religion of Japan. At its holy shrines, people pray for happiness and to honour their ancestors.

... DIWALI? This is the time in the autumn when Hindus celebrate their New Year and honour Lakshmi, goddess of good fortune. Candles are lit and people give each other cards and presents.

... HANUKKAH? Hanukkah celebrates the recapture of the temple in Jerusalem in ancient times. This Jewish festival of light lasts eight days, with families lighting a new candle each day.

... RAMADAN? Ramadan is the ninth month of the Muslim year. During Ramadan, people fast from sunrise to sunset, meaning they don't eat or drink between these times.

... LENT? Lent is the period before Easter that in the Christian Church remembers Jesus Christ's fasting in the wilderness.

... CHRISTMAS? Christmas is the annual Christian festival celebrating Jesus Christ's birth, held on 25 December.

WHAT ARE THE FIVE 'K'S?

Sikh men honour five religious traditions. Kesh is uncut hair, worn in a turban. They carry a Kangha or comb, a Kara or metal bangle, and a Kirpan or dagger. They wear an undergarment called a Kaccha.

WHAT ARE PARSIS?

The Parsis belong to a sect of the Zoroastrian religion, which began long ago in ancient Persia, now Iran. Today, Parsis live in India and Pakistan.

... A POW-WOW?

It means 'a get-together'. The Native American peoples of the United States and the First Nations of Canada meet up at pow-wows each year to celebrate their traditions with dance and music.

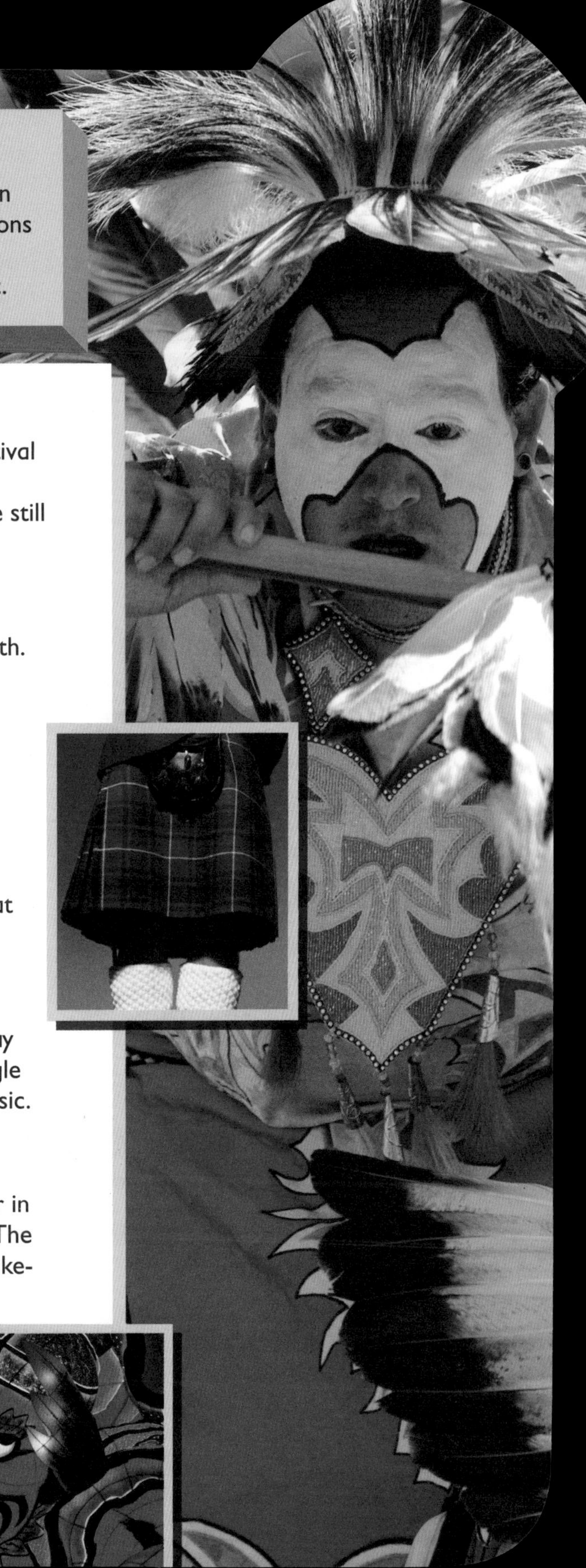

... CARNIVAL?

In ancient Rome there was a rowdy winter festival called Saturnalia. People copied this idea in the Middle Ages, feasting before Lent began. People still celebrate Carnival today.

... BATIK?

Batik is a way of making pretty patterns on cloth. Wax is put on the fibre so that the dye sinks in only in certain places. Batik was invented in Southeast Asia.

...A KILT?

The kilt is a knee-length skirt based on traditional male dress in the Highlands of Scotland. Kilts are woven in tartan patterns that are linked with particular families or regions.

... MORRIS DANCING?

Morris dancing is an English folk dance that may date back to the 15th century. The dancers jingle bells tied to their legs in time to traditional music.

... KABUKI?

Kabuki is a type of drama that became popular in Japan in the 1600s and can still be seen today. The actors, who are always male, wear splendid make-up and costumes.

WHY IS MOUNT ATHOS IMPORTANT?

Mount Athos is a rocky headland in northern Greece, holy to Christians of the Eastern Orthodox faith. Monks have worshipped there since the Middle Ages.

WHY DO SOME PEOPLE LIVE IN CARAVANS?

Many of Europe's Roma people live in caravans, moving from one campsite to another. The Roma, who are sometimes called Gypsies, arrived in Europe from India about 500 years ago.

WHY DO PEOPLE FAST?

In many religions people fast, or go without food, as part of their worship.

WHY DO SOME MONKS COVER THEIR MOUTHS?

Some monks of the Jain religion, in India, wear masks over their mouths. This is because they respect all living things and do not wish to harm or swallow even the tiniest insect that might fly into their mouths.

WHY DO SOME LADIES WEAR TALL LACE HATS?

The Breton people of northwest France are proud of their costume, which they wear for special occasions. Men wear waistcoats and big black hats, while women wear lace caps.

WHY MIGHT PEOPLE THROW PAINT?

During the Hindu festival of Holi, people celebrate the triumph of good over evil by throwing multicoloured water over each other.

WHY DO PEOPLE LIVE IN TENTS?

Many people do not live in the same place all year round, instead following their sheep or goats from one pasture to another. These people are called nomads. The Bedouin are nomads who live in North Africa.

WHY DO PEOPLE LIVE UNDERGROUND?

To stay cool! At Coober Pedy in Australia it is so hot that miners built houses and even a church underground.

WHY BUILD REED HOUSES?

Tall reeds grow around Lake Titicaca in Peru – so the Indians who live there use them to build their houses.

WHY ARE HOUSES BUILT ON STILTS?

In many parts of the world, homes are built on stilts to protect them from flooding or to keep out animals.

WHERE DO PILGRIMS GO?

Pilgrims are religious people who travel to holy places around the world. Muslims try to travel to the sacred city of Mecca, in Saudi Arabia, at least once in their lifetime. Hindus may travel to the city of Varanasi, in India, to wash in the holy waters of the River Ganges. Some Christians travel to Bethlehem, the birthplace of Jesus Christ.

WHICH CITY IS HOLY TO THREE FAITHS?

Jerusalem is a holy place for Jews, Muslims and Christians. Sacred sites include the Western Wall, the Dome of the Rock and the Church of the Holy Sepulchre.

WHERE DO YOUNG BOYS BECOME MONKS?

In Burma a four-year-old boy learns about the life of Buddha at a special ceremony. He is dressed as a rich prince and is then given the simple robes of a Buddhist monk.

WHEN ARE MUSLIMS ALLOWED SWEETS?

The Muslim festival of Eid-ul-Fitr marks the end of a month's fasting during Ramadan. People send special cards, and children enjoy eating traditional sweets.

WHICH COUNTRY HAS THE MOST MUSLIMS?

Indonesia is the largest Islamic country in the world, although some parts of it, such as the island of Bali, are mostly Hindu.

WHO...

...WEARS GREEN ON ST PATRICK'S DAY? St Patrick's Day, on 17 March, is the national day of Ireland. It is celebrated all over the world, wherever Irish people have settled.

... EATS SPIDERS? Spiders are a delicacy in Cambodia. The tastiest are plucked straight from their burrow and fried with lashings of garlic and salt.

...ARE THE TRUE CLOGGIES? A hundred years ago wooden shoes, or clogs, were worn in many parts of Europe. The most famous clogs were Dutch, and are still worn today by farmers and market traders in the Netherlands.

... GETS TO SIT IN THE LEADER'S CHAIR? In Turkey, 23 April is Children's Day. One child gets the chance to sit at the desk of the country's prime minister!

... RIDES TO THE FERIA? Each April the people of Seville, in Spain, ride on horseback to a fair by the River Guadalquivir. They wear traditional finery and dance all night.

... DANCES A HAKA?
Maori people in New Zealand dance the haka, traditionally danced by warriors to bring them strength to face battle.

... REMEMBERS THE FIFTH OF NOVEMBER?
People in Great Britain. The date recalls the capture of Guy Fawkes, who plotted to blow up the Houses of Parliament in London in 1605. The night is marked by fireworks and bonfires.

... WEARS FEATHERS TO A SINGSING? A singsing is a big festival in Papua New Guinea. Men paint their faces and wear ornaments of bone and shell and long bird-of-paradise feathers.

... PLAYS THE PANS? People in the Caribbean play the 'pans', or steel drums, at Carnival time.

... EATS THE MOST CHEESE? The Greeks eat the most cheese, with the average person consuming 22 kilograms every year. Three-quarters of this is feta cheese, made from ewe's and goat's milk.

... INVENTED NOODLES? Some people say that the traveller Marco Polo brought the secret of noodle-making back to Italy from China in the Middle Ages. Others say the Romans were making pasta in Italy long before that.

... SINGS IN BEIJING? Beijing opera is a spectacular performance. Musicians clash cymbals and actors sing in high voices. With painted faces and beautiful costumes, they take the part of heroes and villains in ancient Chinese tales.

... WROTE A POEM TO HIS HAGGIS? Robert Burns, the great Scottish poet. The haggis is a traditional Scottish dish made of lamb's heart, liver and lungs, suet, onions and oatmeal, all cooked inside a sheep's stomach.

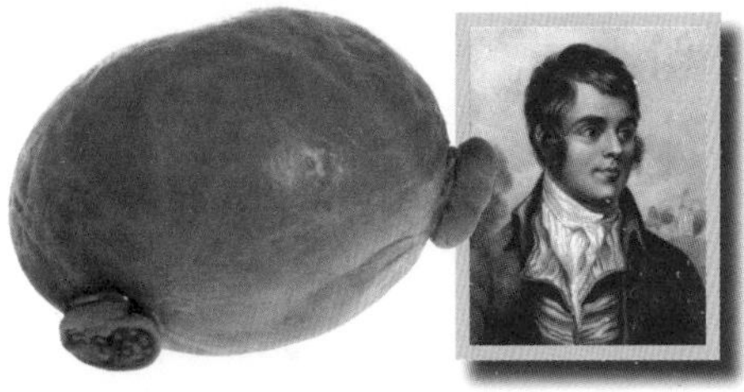

... PAINTS THE DREAMTIME? Australia's Aboriginals look back to the Dreamtime, a magical age when the world was being formed. Many paintings show the landscape and how it was moulded by animals.

... MAKES PICTURES FROM SAND? The Navajo people of the southwestern United States make beautiful patterns using many different coloured sands.

WHAT ARE HOUSES MADE FROM?

Mud, stone, slate, boulders, bricks, branches, reeds, steel girders, sheets of iron, concrete, glass, timber, straw, turf, ice, bamboo, animal hides, cardboard boxes – you name it!

WHY DO CHALETS HAVE BIG ROOFS?

In the mountains of Switzerland, the wooden houses have broad roofs, designed to cope with heavy falls of snow each winter.

HOW DO PEOPLE DRESS IN HOT COUNTRIES?

In hot countries people protect their heads from the sun with broad-brimmed hats, from the Mexican sombrero to the cone-shaped hats worn by farm workers in southern China and Vietnam.

WHAT ARE CLOTHES MADE FROM?

Clothes today may be made from natural fibres, such as wool or cotton, or from artificial fibres such as nylon and plastic.

WHO INVENTED SILK?

The Chinese were the first people to make silk, from the cocoons of silkworms, thousands of years ago. Today silk may be used to make bright Indian wraps called saris and Japanese robes called kimonos.

WHAT ARE HOUSES LIKE IN THE ARCTIC?

Today the Inuit people of Canada live in houses, huts and tents. Traditionally, they lived in igloos made out of blocks of snow. Igloos are still used today by Inuits on the move.

WHO MAKES THE WORLD'S HOTTEST CURRIES?

The people of southern India. A mouthwatering recipe might include fiery spices such as red chilli pepper and fresh hot green chillies, ginger, garlic, turmeric and curry leaves.

CAN YOU EAT SEAWEED?

Various seaweeds are eaten in Japan, and in South Wales seaweed makes up a dish called laverbread. A seaweed called carrageen moss is often used to thicken ice cream and milk puddings.

WHAT IS SUSHI?

Sushi is considered a great delicacy in Japan. It is rice wrapped in sheets of seaweed and topped with meat, fish or vegetables.

HOW DO YOU EAT WITH CHOPSTICKS?

Chopsticks are popular in China and Japan. They can be used by holding them between the thumb and fingers in one hand.

WHERE...

... DO THEY DANCE LIKE THE GODS?

Kathakali is a kind of dance-drama performed in Kerala, southern India. Dancers in make-up and costumes act out ancient tales of gods and demons.

... ARE THERE 3 MILLION WORKS OF ART?

At St Petersburg in Russia, in an art gallery made up of two great buildings, the Hermitage and the Winter Palace.

... DO DRAGONS DANCE?

At Chinese New Year or Spring Festival, a dragon weaves along the street, held up by people crouching underneath it.

... DO SOLDIERS WEAR SKIRTS?

Guards of honour in the Greek army are called Evzónes. Their uniform is based on the old-fashioned costume of the mountain peoples – a white skirt, woollen leggings and a cap with a tassel.

... DO PANAMA HATS COME FROM?

They were first made in Ecuador, plaited from the leaves of the toquilla palm. But they were first exported, or shipped abroad, from Panama.

... IS THE CAPITAL OF FASHION?

Paris, in France, has been the centre of world fashion for hundreds of years. Milan, London, New York and other cities also stage fashion shows.

... DO DRUMS TALK?

In Senegal and Gambia, in Africa, the tama is nicknamed the 'talking drum'. Its tightness can be varied while it is being played, making a strange throbbing sound.

... DO YOU BUY MILK BY WEIGHT?

In the Russian Arctic it is so cold in winter that milk is sold in frozen chunks rather than by the litre.

... WERE THE FIRST SKYSCRAPERS BUILT?

High-rise flats and offices were first built in Chicago, USA, about 120 years ago.

... IS STRATFORD?

Stratford-upon-Avon, in England, was the home of the great playwright, William Shakespeare.

... IS THE BLUE CITY?

In Jodhpur, India, many of the houses are painted blue. Inhabitants believe the colour reflects heat and keeps away mosquitoes.

... DO THEY BUILD MUD HUTS?

Thatched huts with walls of dried mud can still be seen in parts of Africa, such as Mali. They are cheap to build and cool to live in.

... IS THE WORLD'S OLDEST THEATRE?

The oldest theatre building still in use is probably the Teatro Olimpico, in Vicenza, Italy. It opened over 400 years ago.

... IS NEW YEAR'S DAY ALWAYS WET?

In Burma, people celebrate the Buddhist New Year by splashing and spraying water over their friends!

... DO PEOPLE LIVE IN FAIRY CHIMNEYS?

In Cappadocia, in eastern Turkey, people have carved homes out of natural cone-shaped rock formations known as 'fairy chimneys'.

WHY WAS...

ANCIENT EGYPT SO GREAT?

Ancient Egypt was one of the greatest civilizations in history. It grew up along the Nile River, in northeast Africa. Under the rule of kings known as pharaohs, the Egyptians made great leaps of progress in building, art and science. Many of their monuments and tombs are still standing today, some 4,000 years later!

HOW OLD ARE THE PYRAMIDS?

The first pyramid was built between 2630 and 2611 BC. It had stepped sides and was built for King Djoser. Before then, pharaohs were buried in flat-topped mounds called mastabas. The last pyramid in Egypt itself was built about 1530 BC.

HOW WAS A PYRAMID BUILT?

By man-power! Thousands of labourers worked in the hot sun to clear the site, lay the foundations, drag building stone from the quarry and lift it into place. Most of the labourers were ordinary farmers, who worked as builders to pay their dues to the pharaoh. Expert craftsmen cut the stone into blocks and fitted them together.

WHY WERE PYRAMIDS BUILT?

The pyramids are huge tombs for pharaohs and wealthy people. The Egyptians believed that dead people's spirits could live on after death if their bodies were carefully preserved. It was specially important to preserve the bodies of dead pharaohs as their spirits would help the kingdom of Egypt to survive. So they made dead bodies into mummies, and buried them in these splendid tombs along with clothes and jewels.

WHAT IS A MUMMY?

A mummy is the body of a person or animal that has been preserved after death.

WHY DID EGYPTIANS TREASURE SCARABS?

Scarabs (beetles) collect animal dung and roll it into little balls. To the Egyptians, these dung balls looked like the life-giving Sun, so they hoped that scarabs would bring them long life.

HOW WERE CORPSES MUMMIFIED?

Making a mummy was a complicated and expensive process. First, the soft internal organs were removed, then the body was packed in chemicals and left to dry out. Finally, it was wrapped in bandages and placed in a decorated coffin.

WHY WAS THE NILE RIVER SO IMPORTANT?

Because Egypt got hardly any rain. But every year the Nile flooded the fields along its banks, bringing fresh water and rich black silt, which helped crops grow. The river was also vital for transporting people and goods.

WHAT ARE FELUCCAS?

Feluccas are traditional wooden boats that have sailed on the Nile for thousands of years.

WHY DO WE LEARN ABOUT ANCIENT GREECE?

From the 8th century BC, a great civilization began to grow in Greece, allowing architects, thinkers and artists to thrive.

WHY DID GREEK TEMPLES HAVE SO MANY COLUMNS?

The style may have been copied from ancient Greek palaces, which had lots of wooden pillars to hold up the roof.

WHO WAS APHRODITE?

Aphrodite was the Greek goddess of love.

WHY DID THE GREEKS BUILD SO MANY TEMPLES?

Because they worshipped so many different goddesses and gods! The Greeks believed each god needed a home where its spirit could live. Every god had special powers, which visitors to the temple prayed for.

WHAT WAS SPECIAL ABOUT GREEK ARCHITECTURE?

Greek architecture was based on balance and order.

WHAT WERE THE ORIGINAL OLYMPIC GAMES?

In 776 BC, the Greeks set up an athletics competition in the city of Olympia. It was held every four years. Athletes travelled from all over Greece to compete.

DID THE ROMANS HAVE CENTRAL HEATING?

Yes. They invented a system called the 'hypocaust'. Air heated by a wood-burning furnace was circulated through pipes underneath the floor.

WHO WAS ZEUS?

According to the ancient Greeks, Zeus was the god of the sky.

WHY DID THE ROMAN EMPEROR HADRIAN BUILD A WALL?

By the 3rd century BC, the Romans controlled an empire from Britain to North Africa. To help guard its frontiers, Emperor Hadrian ordered a wall to be built across the north of Britain.

WHO WERE ROMAN CENTURIONS?

Centurions were army officers. They wore a decorated metal breastplate and a helmet topped with a crest of horsehair.

WHO WERE THE VIKINGS?

The Vikings came from Norway, Denmark and Sweden. From around AD 800 until AD 1100, they made raids across Europe, killing, burning and carrying away their loot. Not all Vikings were raiders, however. Some travelled to new places to settle, and many were hunters and farmers who never left home.

WERE THE VIKINGS GOOD SAILORS?

Yes. They sailed for thousands of kilometres across the icy northern oceans in open wooden boats, known as longboats.

WHAT DOES 'VIKING' MEAN?

The word 'Viking' comes from the old Scandinavian word *vik*, which means a narrow bay beside the sea.

WHAT GODS DID VIKINGS BELIEVE IN?

The Vikings prayed to many different gods. Thor sent thunder and protected craftsmen. Odin was the god of wisdom and war. Kindly goddess Freya gave peace and fruitful crops.

WHAT DID VIKINGS SEIZE ON THEIR RAIDS?

All kinds of treasure. A hoard of silver, including coins and belt buckles, was buried by Vikings in the 10th century and discovered in Lancashire, England, in 1840. The Vikings also kidnapped people to sell as slaves.

DID THE VIKINGS REACH AMERICA?

Yes. A bold adventurer named Leif Ericsson sailed from Greenland until he reached 'Vinland' (present-day Newfoundland, Canada). He built a farm but decided to return home after quarrelling with the locals!

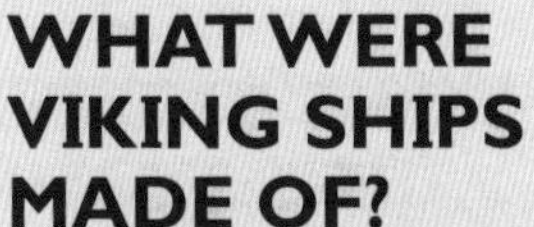

WHAT WERE VIKING SHIPS MADE OF?

Narrow, flexible strips of wood, fixed to a solid wooden backbone called a keel. They were powered by men rowing, or by the wind trapped in big square sails.

WHO BUILT PYRAMIDS TO STUDY THE STARS?

Priests of the Maya civilization, which was powerful in Central America between AD 200 and 900. They built huge, stepped pyramids, with temples and observatories at the top to study astronomy.

WHO WROTE IN PICTURES?

Maya and Aztec scribes in Central and South America. The Maya used a system of picture symbols called glyphs. Maya and Aztecs both wrote in stitched books, called codices, using paper made from bark.

WHO WERE THE AZTECS?

The Aztecs were wandering hunters who arrived in Mexico about AD 1200. They fought against the people already living there, built a city called Tenochtitlan, and soon grew rich and strong.

WHEN WERE THE MIDDLE AGES?

When historians talk about the Middle Ages, or the Medieval period, they usually mean the time from the collapse of the Roman Empire, around AD 500, to about 1500.

WHAT IS ISLAM? The religious faith taught by the Prophet Muhammad, who lived in Arabia from AD 570 to 632. People who follow the faith of Islam are called Muslims.

WHEN DID THE ISLAMIC WORLD LEAD THE GLOBE? From about AD 700 to 1200, the Islamic World experienced a period of great power. It led the rest of the globe in learning, invention and architecture.

WHAT WERE THE CRUSADES? A series of wars fought between Christian and Muslim soldiers for control of the area around Jerusalem. The Crusades began in AD 1095 and ended in 1291, when Muslim soldiers forced the Christians to leave.

WHO WERE THE MONGOLS? They were nomads who roamed over Central Asia. In AD 1206, the Mongol tribes united under a leader known as Genghis Khan and set out to conquer the world.

WHO WERE THE INCAS?

A people who lived in the Andes Mountains of South America (part of present-day Peru and Ecuador). They ruled a mighty empire from the early 15th century to early 16th century.

HOW DID THE MAYA, AZTECS AND INCAS LOSE THEIR POWER?

They were conquered by soldiers from Spain, who arrived in America in the early 16th century, looking for gold.

WHY WERE LLAMAS SO IMPORTANT?

Because they could survive in the Incas' mountain homeland, where it is cold and windy, and few plants grow. The Incas wove cloth from llama wool and used llamas to carry loads up steep paths.

WHAT MADE CHINA SO RICH?

In the Middle Ages, the Chinese made great strides in agriculture, digging irrigation channels and building new machines. Meanwhile, the emperor ruled China effectively, allowing it to become rich.

WHAT WAS CHINA'S BEST-KEPT SECRET?

How to make silk. For centuries, no one else knew how to do this.

WHERE WAS THE MIDDLE KINGDOM? The Chinese believed their country was at the centre of the world, so they called it the Middle Kingdom.

WHO FARMED LAND THEY DID NOT OWN? Poor peasant families. Under Medieval law, all land belonged to the king, or to rich nobles. The peasants lived in little cottages in return for rent or for work on the land.

WHO DID BATTLE IN METAL SUITS? Kings, lords and knights in Europe during the Middle Ages. From about AD 1000, knights wore simple chain-mail tunics, but by about 1450, armour was made of shaped metal plates.

WHICH RUSSIAN TSAR WAS TERRIBLE? Ivan IV became tsar of Russia in 1533 and was known as Ivan the Terrible. He was clever but ruthless and killed everyone who opposed him.

WHO WAS THE VIRGIN QUEEN? Elizabeth I of England, who reigned from 1558 to 1603. Under her leadership, England grew stronger. She never married and ruled alone.

WHICH KINGS BUILT TALL TOWERS?

Shona kings of southeast Africa, who built a city called Great Zimbabwe. Zimbabwe means 'stone houses'. The city was also a massive fortress. From inside this fortress, the Shona kings ruled a rich empire from AD 1100 to 1600.

WHO BUILT CASTLES AND CATHEDRALS?

Kings, queens and nobles. The first castles were wooden forts. Later, they were built of stone. Cathedrals were very big churches, in cities or towns. They were built to reflect God's glory and to bring honour to those who had paid for them.

WHO BUILT THE TAJ MAHAL?

The Mughal emperor Shah Jahan (ruled 1628–58). He was so sad when his wife Mumtaz Mahal died that he built a lovely tomb for her, called the Taj Mahal. It is made of pure white marble decorated with gold and semi-precious stones.

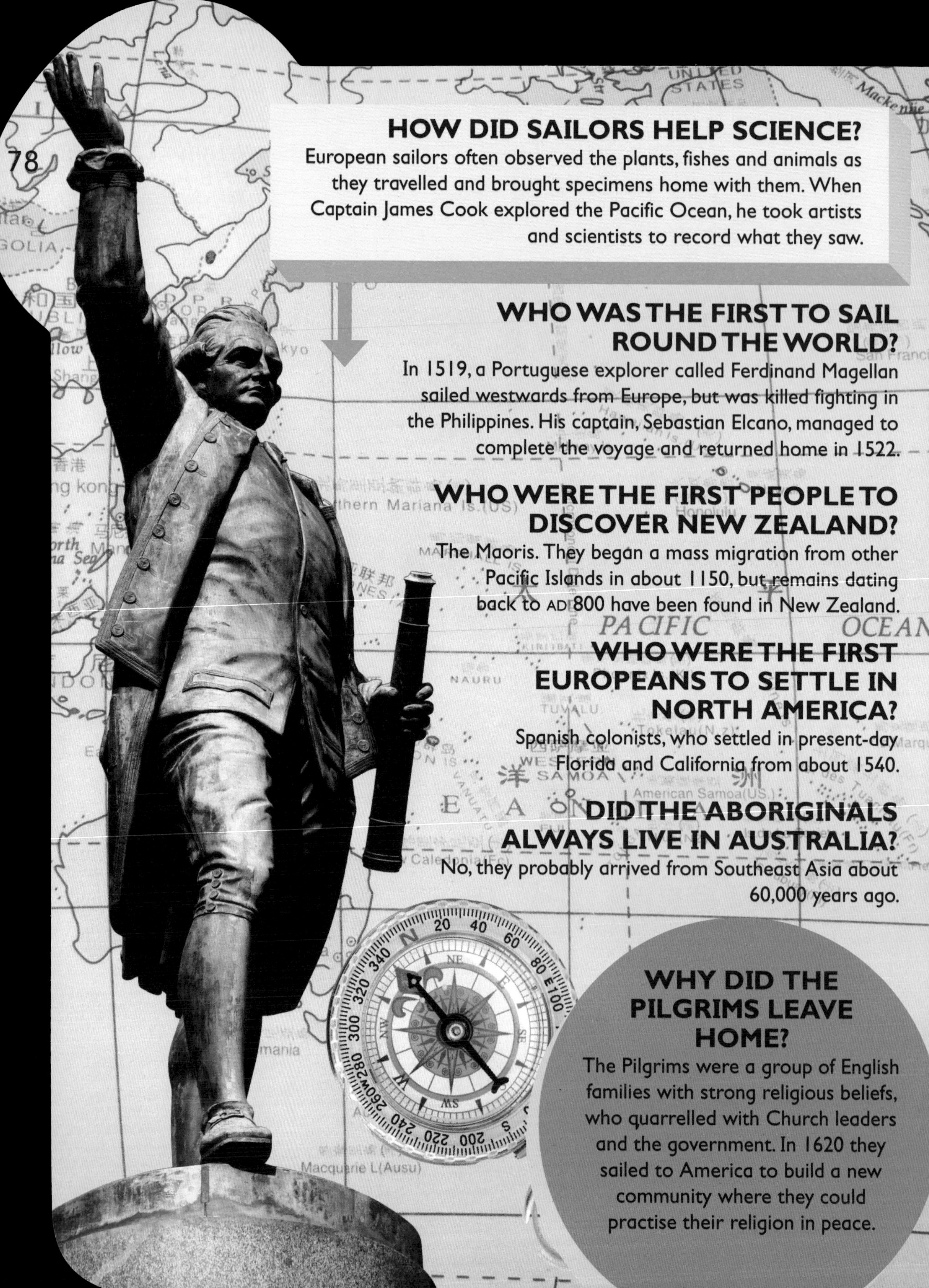

HOW DID SAILORS HELP SCIENCE?

European sailors often observed the plants, fishes and animals as they travelled and brought specimens home with them. When Captain James Cook explored the Pacific Ocean, he took artists and scientists to record what they saw.

WHO WAS THE FIRST TO SAIL ROUND THE WORLD?

In 1519, a Portuguese explorer called Ferdinand Magellan sailed westwards from Europe, but was killed fighting in the Philippines. His captain, Sebastian Elcano, managed to complete the voyage and returned home in 1522.

WHO WERE THE FIRST PEOPLE TO DISCOVER NEW ZEALAND?

The Maoris. They began a mass migration from other Pacific Islands in about 1150, but remains dating back to AD 800 have been found in New Zealand.

WHO WERE THE FIRST EUROPEANS TO SETTLE IN NORTH AMERICA?

Spanish colonists, who settled in present-day Florida and California from about 1540.

DID THE ABORIGINALS ALWAYS LIVE IN AUSTRALIA?

No, they probably arrived from Southeast Asia about 60,000 years ago.

WHY DID THE PILGRIMS LEAVE HOME?

The Pilgrims were a group of English families with strong religious beliefs, who quarrelled with Church leaders and the government. In 1620 they sailed to America to build a new community where they could practise their religion in peace.

WHO LIVED IN TENTS ON THE GREAT PLAINS?

Native American hunters, like the Sioux and the Cheyenne. After Europeans settled in America, bringing horses with them, Native Americans spent summer on the grasslands of the Great Plains, following herds of buffalo, which they killed for meat and skins. In winter, they camped in sheltered valleys.

WHAT STORIES DO TOTEM POLES TELL?

Native American people who lived in the forests of northwest North America carved tall totem poles to record their family's history and to re-tell ancient legends about powerful spirits.

WHEN DID THE USA BECOME INDEPENDENT?

On 4 July, 1776, 13 English colonies (where most Europeans in America had settled) made a Declaration of Independence, refusing to be ruled by Britain any longer. They became a new nation, the United States of America.

WHY DID A CIVIL WAR BREAK OUT?

The American Civil War (1861–65), between the northern and southern states, was caused mainly by a quarrel over slavery. The southern states relied on African slaves working in their cotton plantations. The northern states wanted slavery banned. After four years, the northern states won and slavery was abolished.

WHAT WAS THE INDUSTRIAL REVOLUTION?

The Industrial Revolution was a huge change in the way people worked and goods were produced. Machines in large factories replaced craftspeople working by hand. It began around 1750 in Britain and spread slowly to Western Europe and the USA.

WHY WAS STEAM POWER SO IMPORTANT? A steam engine can do work – such as powering machines or trains – using hot steam. Steam power allowed quicker production of goods in factories and swift transport to buyers.

WHAT WAS THE GREAT EXHIBITION? It was a chance for Britain to show off its industrial achievements. Held in London in 1851, it was viewed by 6 million visitors from around the world.

WHAT WAS THE GREAT STINK? It was a time during the summer of 1858 when London smelled particularly bad. Stinky sewage filled the streets and river.

WHEN DID THE FIRST TRAINS RUN? The first passenger railway was opened in the north of England in 1825. Its locomotives were powered by steam and replaced horse-drawn railway wagons.

WHAT WAS STEPHENSON'S ROCKET? In 1829, the railway engineer George Stephenson built a groundbreaking steam locomotive, called the Rocket.

WHO WORKED IN THE FIRST FACTORIES? Thousands of poor men and women moved from the countryside to live in factory towns. They hoped to find regular work and more pay.

DID CHILDREN LEAD BETTER LIVES THEN? No. Many worked 16 hours a day in factories or down mines. Many were killed in accidents with machinery.

HOW DID THE RAILWAYS CHANGE PEOPLE'S LIVES? They carried materials to factories and finished goods to shops. They also carried fresh foods from farms to cities and made it easier for people to travel.

WHO FOUGHT AND DIED IN THE TRENCHES?

Millions of young men during the First World War (1914–18). Trenches were ditches dug into the ground. They were meant to shelter soldiers from gunfire, but offered little protection from shells exploding overhead. The trenches filled with mud, water, rats and dead bodies.

WHO TOOK PART IN THE SPACE RACE?

The USSR and the USA. Each tried to rival the other's achievements in space. The USSR took the lead by launching the first satellite in 1957, but America landed the first man on the Moon in 1969.

WHO DROPPED THE FIRST ATOMIC BOMB?

On 6 August, 1945, the USA bombed Hiroshima in Japan, killing 66,000 people instantly. Days later, Japan surrendered, ending the Second World War.

WHAT WAS THE COLD WAR?

A time of tension from the 1940s to the 1980s between the USA and the USSR. The USA believed in capitalism; the USSR was communist. The superpowers never fought face to face, but their distrust drew them into local conflicts around the globe.

WHO MADE FIVE YEAR PLANS?

Joseph Stalin, the Russian communist leader who ruled from 1929 to 1953. He reorganized the country in a series of Five Year Plans. He built thousands of new factories, took land from ordinary people and divided it into vast collective farms. Critics of his policies were often killed.

WHAT IS...

AN ELEMENT?

An element is a substance that cannot be split into other substances. Water is not an element because it can be split into the gases oxygen and hydrogen. Oxygen and hydrogen are elements because they cannot be split.

WHAT IS...

...A MOLECULE?	A molecule is the smallest part of a substance that can exist on its own.
... A PROTON?	A particle inside an atom's nucleus. It has a positive electrical charge.
... A NEUTRON?	Another kind of particle inside the nucleus. It has no electrical charge.
... AN ELECTRON?	Negatively electrically charged particles inside a nucleus.
... AN ELECTRON SHELL?	Electrons are stacked around the nucleus at different levels or 'shells'.
... ATOMIC NUMBER?	Every element has its own atomic number. This is the number of protons in its nucleus, balanced by the same number of electrons.
... ATOMIC MASS?	Atomic mass is the 'weight' of one whole atom of a substance. It includes both protons and neutrons.
...THE PERIODIC TABLE?	Elements can be ordered into a chart called the periodic table. Columns are called groups; rows are called periods.
... THE LIGHTEST ELEMENT?	The lightest element is hydrogen. It has an atomic mass of just one.
... A NOBLE GAS?	The noble gases do not easily react with other elements.

HOW BIG ARE ATOMS?

Atoms are about a ten millionth of a millimetre across and weigh 100 trillionths of a trillionth of a gram. The smallest atom is hydrogen; the largest is ununoctium.

CAN ATOMS JOIN TOGETHER?

Yes! Electrons are held to the nucleus by electrical attraction, because they have an opposite electrical charge to the protons in the nucleus. But electrons can also be drawn to the nuclei of other atoms. This is when bonding takes place.

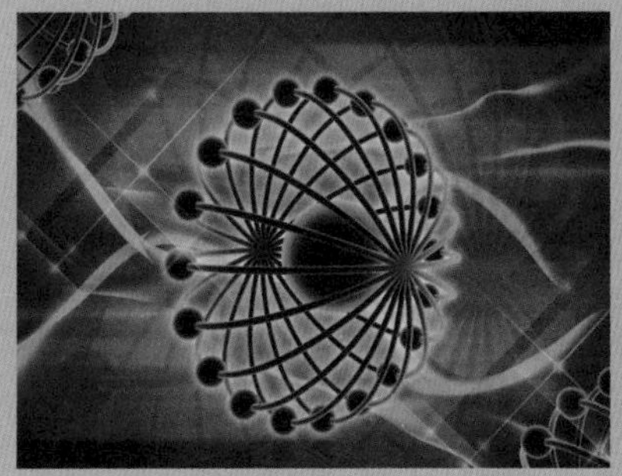

HOW MANY ELEMENTS ARE THERE?

New elements are sometimes discovered, but the total number identified so far is 118.

WHAT IS THE SMALLEST PARTICLE?

No one is sure. Atoms are made of protons, neutrons and electrons. In turn, these are made of even tinier particles – quarks and leptons. Scientists know about more than 200 kinds of sub-atomic particles so far.

WHY ARE SOME ELEMENTS REACTIVE?

Elements are reactive if they readily gain or lose electrons. Elements on the left of the periodic table, called metals, lose electrons very easily. The farther left they are, the more reactive they are.

WHAT ARE...

... SUBSTANCES?

Substances can be solids, liquids or gases. Substances move from one state of matter to another when they are heated or cooled, boosting or reducing the energy of their particles.

... LIQUIDS?

In liquids, particles move around a bit, so liquids can flow into any shape, while their volume stays the same.

... SOLIDS?

In solids, particles are locked together, so solids have a definite shape and volume.

... GASES?

In gases, particles zoom about all over the place, so gases spread out to fill containers of any size or shape. Gases can expand and contract depending on pressure and temperature.

WHAT HAPPENS IN EVAPORATION?

Evaporation happens when a liquid is warmed up and changes to a vapour. Particles at the liquid's surface vibrate so fast they escape altogether.

WHAT HAPPENS IN CONDENSATION?

Condensation happens when a vapour is cooled down and becomes liquid. Evaporation and condensation take place not only at boiling point, but also at much cooler temperatures.

WHEN DO THINGS BOIL?

Things boil from liquid to gas when they reach boiling point, which is the maximum temperature a liquid can reach. For water this is 100°C.

WHEN DO THINGS MELT?

Things melt from solid to liquid on reaching a temperature called the melting point. Each substance has its own melting point. Water's is 0°C; lead's is 327.5°C.

WHEN DO THINGS FREEZE?

Things freeze from liquid to solid when they reach the freezing point.

WHAT IS PLASMA?

Plasma is the fourth state of matter. It occurs only when a gas becomes so hot its atoms and molecules collide and electrons are ripped free. Plasma displays, in which the plasma emits light, are used for many television screens.

WHO...

... DISCOVERED RADIUM?

The Polish-French physicist Marie Curie (1867–1934) was the first woman to win not one, but two, Nobel Prizes. The first, in 1903, was for her part in the discovery of radioactivity, and the second, in 1911, for her discovery of the elements polonium and radium.

... FIRST SPLIT THE ATOM?

In 1919, the physicist Ernest Rutherford managed to break down nitrogen atoms into hydrogen and oxygen. In 1932, his students John Cockcroft and Ernest Walton managed to split the nucleus of an atom by firing protons at it.

... WAS HANS GEIGER?

Hans Geiger (1882–1945) was a German physicist who contributed towards the invention of the Geiger counter. The counter measures radioactivity by detecting alpha, beta and gamma rays.

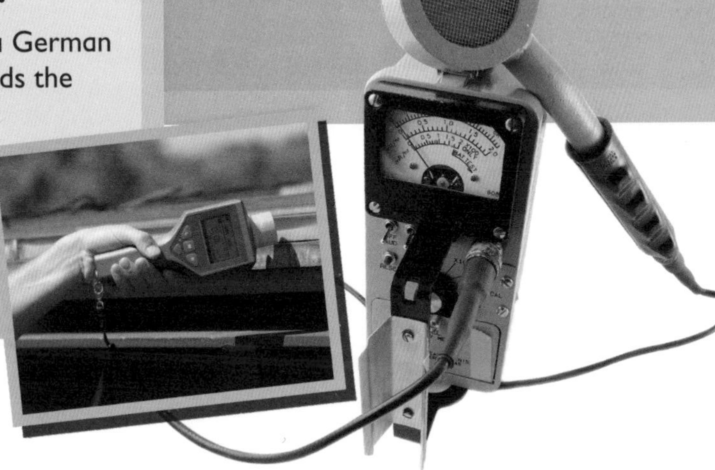

... DISCOVERED THE SHAPE OF DNA?

The discovery in 1953 that every molecule of DNA is shaped like a twisted rope ladder, or 'double helix', was one of the great scientific breakthroughs of the 20th century. Maurice Wilkins and Rosalind Franklin did the groundwork for the discovery. Francis Crick and James Watson, two young researchers at Cambridge University, UK, had the inspiration and won the Nobel Prize.

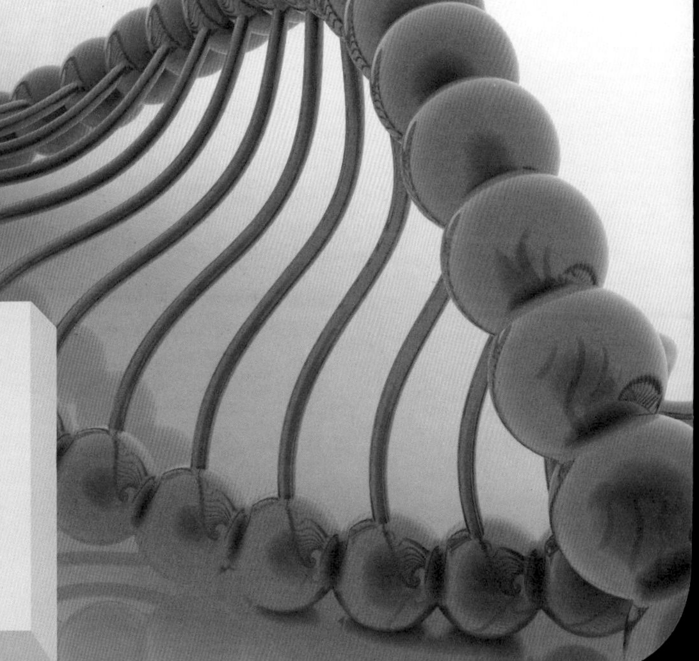

... INVENTED THE ATOMIC BOMB?

The first atomic bombs were developed in the USA towards the end of the Second World War by a team of scientists led by Robert Oppenheimer (1904–1967).

WHAT IS...

... A COMPOUND?	Compounds are substances made from two or more elements joined together.
... A MIXTURE?	Mixtures are substances that contain several chemical elements or compounds mixed together but not chemically joined.
... A METAL?	A metal is hard, dense and shiny, and goes 'ping' when you strike it with another metal. It also conducts, or transfers, electricity and heat well.
... AN ION?	An ion is an atom that has either lost one or a few electrons, or gained a few. Ions usually form when substances dissolve in a liquid.
... ELECTROLYSIS?	Electrolysis is a means of separating compounds by passing an electric current through them.
... PRESSURE?	Pressure is the amount of force pressing on something. Air pressure is the force with which air presses.

HOW...

... DO CHEMICALS REACT?

When substances react chemically, their atoms, ions and molecules interact to form new combinations. Nearly all chemical reactions involve a change in energy, usually heat, as the bonds between particles are broken and formed.

... DOES PRESSURE CHANGE? If you squeeze a gas into half the space, the pressure doubles (as long as the temperature stays the same). This is Boyle's Law. If you warm up a gas, the pressure rises in proportion (as long as you keep it the same volume). This is the Pressure Law.

... DO THINGS DISSOLVE?

When solids dissolve in liquid, it may look as if the solid disappears. Its atoms, ions or molecules are, in fact, still intact – but are separated and evenly dispersed throughout the liquid.

... DO BATTERIES WORK?

Batteries create electric currents from the reaction between two chemicals, one forming a positive electrode, or conductor of electricity, and the other a negative. The reaction creates an excess of electrons on the negative electrode, producing a current.

... DOES BREAD RISE?

Bakers add yeast, a type of fungus, to dough before they put it in the oven. When it is heated, yeast reacts with the sugar in the dough to make carbon dioxide. This gas forms pockets in the bread, making it rise.

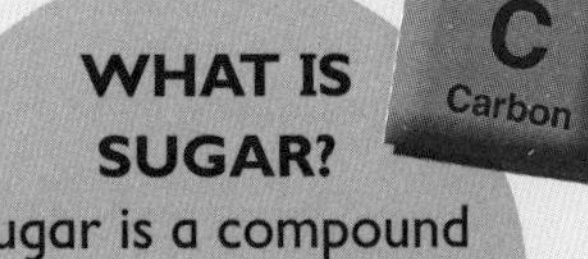

WHAT IS SUGAR?
Sugar is a compound of the elements carbon, hydrogen and oxygen.

WHAT ARE CLOUDS? Clouds form when warm air is heated by the Sun and rises. As it rises, the warm air cools, eventually becoming cold enough for the water vapour it contains to condense into water droplets, which we can see as clouds.

WHAT IS THE SEA MADE OF?
The sea is water with oxygen, carbon dioxide, nitrogen and various salts dissolved in it.

WHAT IS FIRE? Fire is a chemical reaction in which a substance gets so hot that it combines with oxygen in the air. The flames we see are the heat and light energy created by the reaction.

WHAT IS RADIOACTIVITY?

Radioactivity is when the nucleus of an atom is unstable and breaks down, emitting radiation in the form of alpha, beta and gamma rays. These high-energy rays can be dangerous in large doses, causing burns and an increased risk of cancer.

WHAT CAUSES RADIOACTIVITY?

The atoms of an element may come in several different forms, or isotopes. The nuclei of some of these isotopes are unstable and they decay (break up), releasing radiation.

WHICH ELEMENTS ARE VERY RADIOACTIVE?

The actinides are a group of 15 elements at the bottom of the periodic table that take their name from actinium. They include plutonium and uranium.

WHAT IS HALF-LIFE?

No one can predict when an atomic nucleus will decay. But scientists can predict how long it will take for half the atoms in a quantity of a radioactive element to decay. This is its half-life.

WHAT IS NUCLEAR POWER?

The energy that binds together an atomic nucleus is enormous, even though the nucleus is tiny. By harnessing this energy, nuclear power stations can generate huge amounts of power with just a few tonnes of nuclear fuel.

HOW DO NUCLEAR POWER STATIONS WORK?

A nuclear reactor houses fuel rods made from uranium dioxide. A nuclear fission chain reaction is set up in the fuel rods. The resulting energy is used to heat water, which produces steam to drive the turbines, or wheels, that generate electricity.

HOW MUCH ELECTRICITY IS MADE BY NUCLEAR POWER?

Nuclear power produces about 15% of the world's electricity. Some people oppose any further increase in it because its used fuel is very radioactive and hard to dispose of safely.

WHAT IS NUCLEAR FISSION?

Nuclear fission releases nuclear energy by splitting big atomic nuclei, usually those of uranium. Neutrons are fired at the nuclei. As the neutrons smash into the nuclei, they split off more neutrons, which bombard other nuclei, setting off a chain reaction.

WHAT IS NUCLEAR FUSION?

Nuclear energy is released by fusing, or joining together, small atoms like those of a form of hydrogen called deuterium, often in a reactor. Nuclear fusion is the reaction that provides energy for H-bombs. Scientists hope to find a way of harnessing nuclear fusion for power generation.

WHAT IS AN ATOMIC BOMB?

An atomic bomb is a kind of nuclear bomb. It relies on the explosive nuclear fission of uranium-235 or plutonium-239.

WHY...

... IS WATER ESSENTIAL FOR LIFE? Water is a neutral chemical, yet dissolves many substances, which is why it is so important for life. Water is found in every cell of the human body. Plants need water for building cells and also for transporting nutrients.

... DO ICEBERGS FLOAT IN THE SEA? Water is unique – it expands when it freezes because the special bonds between its hydrogen atoms begin to break down. This means that ice is lighter (less dense) than water, so icebergs can float.

... DO THINGS FLOAT?
When an object is immersed in water, its weight pushes it down. But the water around it pushes it back up. An object will float if it is lighter than, or weighs the same as, the water it has pushed out of its way.

... IS WATER SPECIAL?
Water is found naturally as solid ice, liquid water and gaseous water vapour. This is unusual and happens because of the strong bonds between its two hydrogen and one oxygen atom.

WHAT IS HYDROELECTRIC POWER?

Hydroelectric power is electricity generated by turbines turned by falling water.

WHAT IS...

... ORGANIC CHEMISTRY?	Organic chemistry is the study of carbon and its thousands of different compounds.
... DNA?	DNA is deoxyribonucleic acid found inside every living cell. DNA provides the instructions for all the cell's activities and for the life plan of the entire organism.
...A CARBOHYDRATE?	Carbohydrates are chemicals made of carbon, hydrogen and oxygen atoms, including sugars, starches and cellulose. Carbohydrates provide animals with energy.
...A POLYMER?	Polymers are substances made from long chains of carbon-based molecules. Some polymers occur naturally, such as wool and cotton, but plastics such as nylon and polythene are man-made.
...THE CARBON CYCLE?	Animals breathe out carbon as carbon dioxide. Plants take in carbon dioxide from the air and convert it to oxygen. When animals eat plants, they take in carbon again.
...A CARBON CHAIN?	Carbon atoms often link together, like the links of a chain, to form very long, thin molecules.
... CELLULOSE?	Cellulose is a fibre found in the walls of plant cells. It is a polymer and it makes the plant tough and stringy.
... OIL? 	Oil is a thick liquid that won't mix with water. Mineral oils used for motor fuel are called hydrocarbons – complex chemicals made from hydrogen and carbon.

HOW IS PLASTIC MADE?

Most plastics are made from ethene, a product of oil that has been heated under pressure. During the process, ethene molecules join in chains. If the chains are held tightly together, the plastic is stiff. If the chains can slip over each other, the plastic is bendy, like polythene.

HOW IS NATURAL OIL MADE?

Oil is formed from tiny plants and animals that lived in warm seas millions of years ago. As they died, they were slowly buried beneath the seabed. As the seabed sediments hardened, the remains of the organisms turned to oil.

WHAT IS...

ENERGY?

Energy takes many forms. Heat energy boils water, keeps us warm and drives engines. Chemical energy fuels cars. Electrical energy drives machines and keeps lights glowing. Light itself is a form of energy. Almost every form of energy can be converted into other forms. But whatever form it is in, energy is essentially the capacity for making something happen, or 'doing work'.

WHAT IS A FORCE?

A force makes something move, by pushing or pulling it. Gravity is an invisible force. Other forces, such as a kick, we can see. Forces work in pairs. For every force pushing in one direction, there is an equal and opposite force pushing in the opposite direction. A space rocket, for example, must overcome the force of gravity in order to fly into space.

WHAT IS POWER?

Power is the rate at which work is done. A high-powered engine is an engine that can move a great deal of weight very quickly. Power is also the rate at which energy is transferred. A large amount of electric power might be needed to heat a large quantity of water.

WHAT IS FRICTION?

Friction is the force between two things rubbing together, which may be brake pads on a bicycle wheel or air molecules against an aeroplane. Friction slows things down, making them hot as their momentum, or movement, is converted into heat.

WHAT IS...

... MASS?	Mass is the amount of matter in an object. It is the same wherever you measure it, even on the Moon.
...WEIGHT?	Weight is a measure of the force of gravity on an object. It varies according to where you measure it.
... SPEED?	Speed is how fast something is going.
...VELOCITY?	Velocity is how fast something is going and in which direction.
...ACCELERATION?	Acceleration is how fast something gains speed. The larger the force and the lighter the object, the greater the acceleration.
... INERTIA?	Inertia is the tendency of things to stay still unless they are forced to move.
... MOMENTUM?	Momentum is the tendency of things to keep going once they are moving, unless forced to stop or slow.
... A TURNING FORCE?	When something fixed in one place, called a fulcrum, is pushed or pulled elsewhere, it turns around the fulcrum. When you push a door shut, that push is the turning force and the hinge is the fulcrum.
... UNIFORM MOTION?	Uniform motion is when an object carries on travelling at the same speed in the same direction.

...A KNOCK-ON EFFECT?

When two objects collide, their combined momentum remains the same if nothing else interferes. So if one object loses momentum, this momentum must be passed on to the other object, making it move.

WHY DO THINGS GO ROUND?

If only one force is involved, things will always move in a straight line. Things go round when there is more than one force involved. A wheel goes round because there is one force trying to make it move in a straight line and another keeping it the same distance from the axle.

HOW DO THINGS GET MOVING?

Things only move if forced to move. So when something starts moving, there must be a force involved, whether it is visible, like someone pushing, or invisible, like gravity, which makes things fall.

HOW FAST DOES A STONE FALL?

At first a stone falls faster and faster. As the stone's speed accelerates, air resistance increases until it becomes so great that the stone cannot fall any faster. It now continues to fall at the same velocity, called the terminal velocity.

WHAT HAPPENS WITH EVERY ACTION?

For every action, there is an equal and opposite reaction. When you push your legs against water to swim, for instance, the water pushes back on your legs equally hard.

WHERE DOES ENERGY COME FROM?

Nearly all our energy comes from the Sun. We get some directly by using solar power cells to trap the Sun's heat. Most comes indirectly via fossil fuels (coal and oil), which got their energy from the fossilized plants of which they are made.

WHAT IS HEAT?

Heat is a form of energy caused by the movement of molecules. It is created by chemical reactions, such as fire; nuclear reactions, such as in the Sun; and when other forms of energy, such as electrical or mechanical, are converted.

HOW IS TEMPERATURE MEASURED?

Temperature is usually measured with a thermometer. Some thermometers have a metal strip that bends according to how hot it is. But most contain a liquid, such as mercury, in a tube. As it gets warmer, the liquid expands and its level rises in the tube. The level of the liquid indicates the temperature.

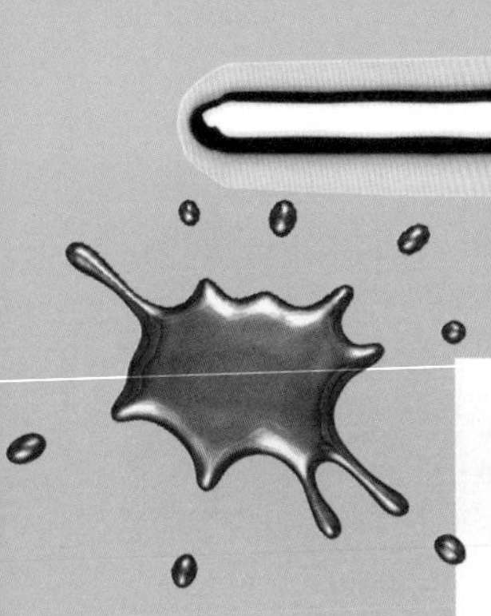

WHAT IS TEMPERATURE?

Temperature is a measure of how fast all the molecules are moving in order to provide heat.

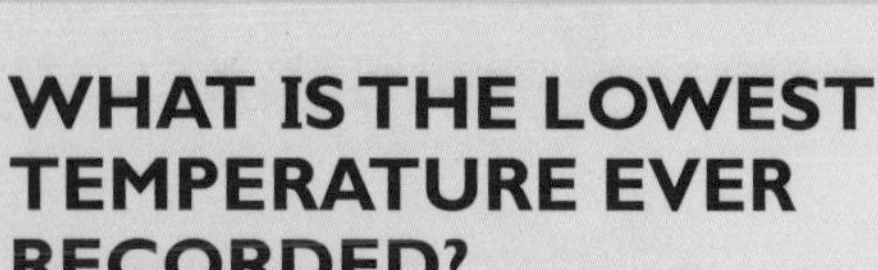

WHAT IS ABSOLUTE ZERO?

Absolute zero is the coldest possible temperature, the temperature at which atoms stop moving altogether. This happens at -273.15°C, or 0 on the Kelvin scale.

WHAT IS THE LOWEST TEMPERATURE EVER RECORDED?

Earth's lowest air temperature ever measured was -89°C. It was recorded in Antarctica. The lowest temperature ever measured was half a billionth of a degree above absolute zero.

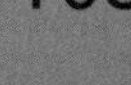

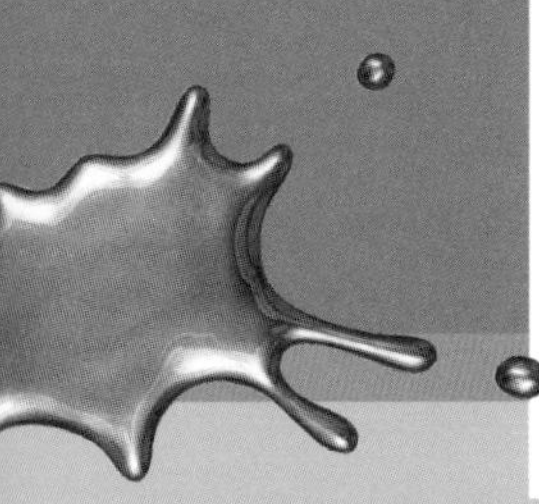

WHAT IS THE HIGHEST TEMPERATURE EVER RECORDED?

The highest temperature ever measured is 2 billion°C. It happened in a nuclear fusion experiment in the USA. The highest air temperature ever recorded is 58°C, in Libya.

HOW DOES THE SUN GENERATE HEAT?

The Sun generates heat by nuclear fusion and radiates it in waves, which we see and feel as sunlight.

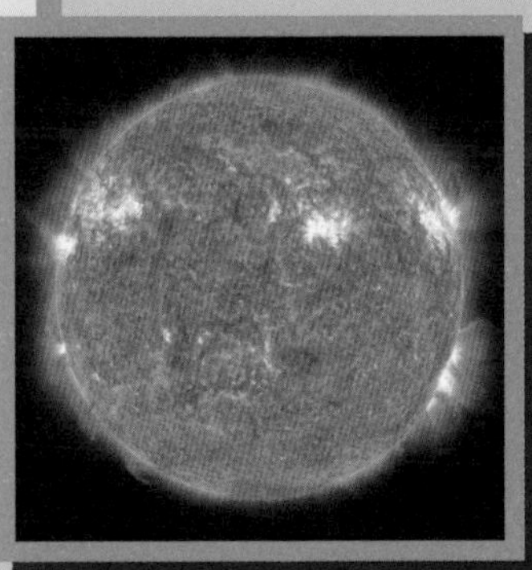

WHY IS MERCURY USED IN THERMOMETERS?

Mercury is one of the few metals that is liquid at room temperature.

HOW DO YOU CONVERT FAHRENHEIT TO CELSIUS?

You can convert from Fahrenheit to Celsius by subtracting 32 then dividing by nine and multiplying by five. You can convert from Celsius to Fahrenheit by dividing by five, multiplying by nine and adding 32.

WHAT IS CONDUCTION?

Conduction is one of the three ways in which heat moves. It involves heat spreading from hot areas to cold areas as moving particles knock into one another. The other ways are convection, in which warm air or water rises, and radiation, which is rays of light.

WHAT IS LIGHT?

There are many sources of light, including the Sun, light bulbs and flames. When light hits an object, it can be reflected, absorbed or bent. The study of light, known as optics, has allowed scientists to discover how we see things.

WHEN IS THE SUN RED?

When the Sun is low in the sky, sunlight reaches us after passing through the dense lower layers of the atmosphere. Particles in the air absorb shorter, bluer wavelengths of light, leaving just the red.

WHAT ARE PHOTONS?

Photons are tiny particles of light. There are billions of them in a single beam of light.

WHAT ARE THE COLOURS OF THE RAINBOW?

The colours of the rainbow are all the colours contained in white light: red, orange, yellow, green, blue, indigo, violet.

WHY IS THE SKY BLUE?

Air molecules reflect more blue from sunlight towards our eyes than the other colours of visible light. This makes the sky appear blue.

WHAT'S THE FASTEST THING IN THE UNIVERSE?

Light, which travels at 300,000 kilometres per second!

HOW DO FIBRE-OPTIC CABLES WORK?

These cables don't bend light, but reflect it round corners. Inside a cable are lots of bundles of glass fibres. Light rays zig-zag along the inside of each fibre, reflecting first off one side, then the other.

HOW DO YOUR EYES SEE THINGS?

The Sun and electric lights shine light rays straight into your eyes. Everything else you see by reflected light, by light rays that bounce off things. So you can see something only if there is a light source throwing light onto it.

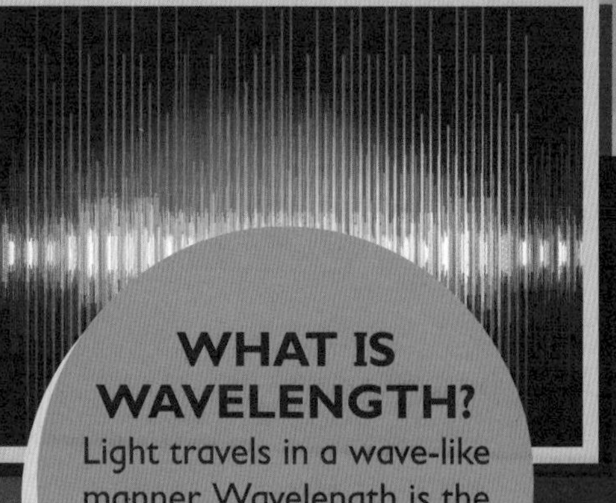

WHAT IS WAVELENGTH?

Light travels in a wave-like manner. Wavelength is the distance between the top of one wave and the next.

WHAT IS INFRARED?

Infrared is light with wavelengths too long for the human eye to register. But you can often feel infrared light as warmth.

HOW IS LIGHT BENT?

Light rays are bent when they are refracted. This happens when they strike a transparent material like glass or water at an angle. The different materials slow the light waves down so that they skew round.

HOW DO OBJECTS ABSORB LIGHT? When light rays hit a surface, some bounce off, but others are absorbed. You see a leaf as green because it has soaked up all the colours except green, and you see only the reflected green light.

DOES LIGHT TRAVEL IN WAVES? Scientists believe light can travel in tiny waves and as bullet-like particles. It is probably best to think of light as vibrating packets of energy.

WHY CAN'T YOU SEE ULTRAVIOLET LIGHT? Ultraviolet light is light with wavelengths too short for the human eye to register.

HOW DO MIRRORS WORK? Most mirrors are made of ordinary glass, but the back is silvered – coated with a shiny metal that reflects all the light that hits it.

WHAT WAS NEWTON'S BREAKTHROUGH?

Sir Isaac Newton's breakthrough, in 1687, was to realize that all movement in the Universe is governed by three simple rules about acceleration, momentum and balancing forces. We call these Newton's Laws of Motion.

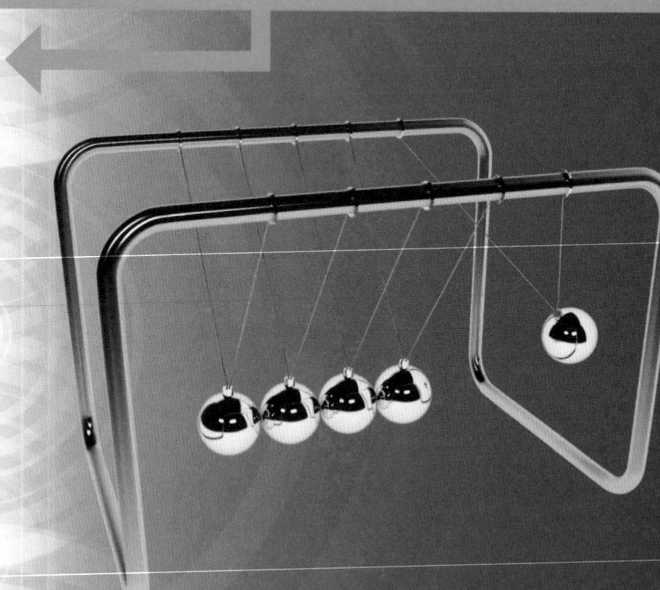

WHO MADE THE FIRST RADIO BROADCAST?

Italian inventor Guglielmo Marconi first sent radio signals over 1,600 metres in 1895. In 1898, he sent a message in Morse code across the English Channel. (Morse code uses rhythms of short and long sounds to represent letters and numerals.) In 1901, he sent a radio message across the Atlantic Ocean.

WHO WAS EINSTEIN?

Albert Einstein (1879–1955) was the genius who transformed science with his two big theories – Special Relativity and General Relativity. The theory of Special Relativity shows how space and time can be measured only relatively – that is, in comparison to something else. This means that time can speed up or slow down, depending on how fast you are moving!

WHAT IS...

Electricity is the presence of electric charge. This charge is carried by electrons and protons in atoms. Electrons have a negative charge and protons a positive one. Electricity can be created naturally, as in lightning, or be man-made, as with a battery.

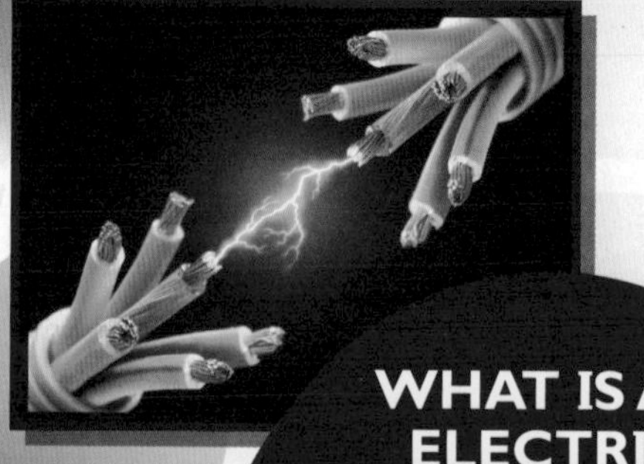

WHAT IS AN ELECTRIC CURRENT?

A current is a continuous stream of electrical charge. It happens only when there is a complete, unbroken 'circuit' for the current to flow through.

HOW DO ELECTRIC CURRENTS FLOW?

The charge in an electric current is electrons that have broken free from their atoms. None of them moves very far, but the current is passed on as they bang into each other like rows of marbles.

WHAT IS A VOLT?

Electrical current flows as long as there is a difference in charge between two points in the circuit. This difference is measured in volts. The bigger the difference, the bigger the voltage.

WHAT IS RESISTANCE?

Resistance is a substance's ability to block a flow of electric current. Insulators, such as the plastic around electrical wires, are used for this reason.

WHAT ARE THE BEST CONDUCTORS?

The best conductors are metals like copper and silver. Water is also a good conductor. Superconductors are materials like aluminium.

ELECTRICITY?

WHAT MAKES LIGHTNING FLASH?

Lightning is created when raindrops and ice crystals inside a thundercloud become electrically charged as they are flung together. Negatively charged particles build up at the cloud's base, then discharge as lightning.

WHAT MAKES YOUR HAIR STAND ON END?

When you comb dry hair, electrons are knocked off the atoms in the comb. Your hair is coated with these negative electrical charges and is attracted to anything positively charged.

HOW DOES A LIGHT BULB WORK?

An electric bulb has a very thin filament of tungsten wire inside a glass bulb filled with argon or nitrogen gas. When current flows through such a thin wire, the resistance is so great that the wire heats up and glows brightly.

WHAT IS A SILICON CHIP?

A silicon chip is an electronic circuit implanted in a small crystal of semiconducting silicon. This led to the manufacture of the microprocessors that make computers work.

WHAT IS MAGNETISM?

Magnetism is a force that both draws together and pushes apart materials. Certain metals can be strongly magnetic. The electrons in every atom act like tiny magnets, attracting and repelling other electrons. Magnetism occurs when the electrons in an object are all aligned in the same direction.

WHAT IS A MAGNETIC FIELD?

A magnetic field is the area around the magnet in which its effects are felt. It gets gradually weaker farther away from the magnet.

WHICH MATERIALS MAKE THE STRONGEST MAGNETS?

Due to the arrangement of their electrons, metals such as iron, nickel and cobalt make strong magnets.

HOW BIG IS THE EARTH'S MAGNETIC FIELD?

The Earth's magnetic field is called the magnetosphere and extends about 70,000 kilometres towards the Sun.

WHAT IS A MAGNETIC POLE?

The two powerful ends of a magnet are called poles. One is called the north pole because if the magnet is suspended freely this pole swings round until it points north.

WHY IS THE EARTH LIKE A MAGNET?

As the Earth spins, the swirling of its iron core turns the core into a giant magnet. Like smaller magnets, the Earth's magnet has two poles, a north and a south.

WHAT IS A LODESTONE?

Lodestones are rocks that contain iron oxide, making them naturally magnetic.

WHAT IS...

... SOUND?	Every sound is created by vibration. Sound reaches your ears as a vibration that travels through the air.
... A SOUND WAVE?	When a sound source vibrates to and fro, it pushes the air around it to and fro in a knock-on effect. This moving stretch and squeeze of air is called a sound wave.
... FREQUENCY?	Sounds differ in pitch depending on the frequency of the sound waves. If the waves follow rapidly after each other, they make a high sound. If they are far apart, they make a low sound.
...VOLUME?	The volume of a sound is the amount of pressure exerted by a sound source on air molecules. The higher the pressure, the harder the molecules will collide and the farther they will travel.
... RESONANCE?	An object tends to vibrate freely at the same rate. This is its natural frequency. If you can keep the object vibrating at the same rate as its natural frequency, the vibrations become stronger. This is resonance.
...AN ECHO?	An example of an echo is when you shout in a tunnel and you hear the noise bouncing back at you a moment later as the sound waves rebound.

WHAT OTHER ANIMALS USE ECHOLOCATION?

Toothed whales, such as porpoises, use echolocation underwater. A porpoise gives off a series of high-pitched clicking sounds and the echoes tell the porpoise where to find its prey.

HOW DO BATS LOCATE THEIR PREY?

Most bats locate their prey using echolocation. The bats send out calls, then use the echoes to locate and identify objects.

WHAT IS...

THE LARGEST LAND ANIMAL?

Elephants are the largest land animals. There are probably three species: the African bush elephant, African forest elephant and Asian elephant. Elephants have tusks, long trunks, flapping ears and very thick skin. After the elephant, the largest land animals are the rhinoceros, hippopotamus and giraffe.

WHAT IS...

... A MAMMAL?	Mammals have backbones, they are hairy and they produce milk to feed their young.
... A PRIMATE?	Primates are mammals that have large brains, hands that can form a good grip and a tendency to walk on two legs.
... AN UNGULATE?	Ungulates are groups of mammals with hoofed feet. They include the rhinoceros, hippopotamus and giraffe.
... A MARSUPIAL?	Marsupials are mammals whose newborns often live in a pouch on their mother's belly.
... A REPTILE?	Reptiles need to breathe air and have skin that is covered in scales.
... A RODENT?	Rodents are mammals with continuously growing incisor teeth, such as squirrels, hamsters and mice.
...A WOMBAT?	A wombat is a small bear-like marsupial with a heavy body and short, strong legs.
...AN OKAPI?	An okapi is a relative of the giraffe that lives in the African rainforest. It does not have a long neck.
...A COYOTE?	The coyote looks similar to a wolf. It lives in North and Central America, where it hunts small mammals.
...A TASMANIAN DEVIL?	The Tasmanian devil is the largest of the flesh-eating marsupials. It is about 90 centimetres long.

...A DINGO?
Dingoes are Australian wild dogs. They hunt mainly sheep and rabbits.

WHAT DO KANGAROOS EAT?

Kangaroos eat grass and the leaves of low-growing plants, just like deer and antelopes do in the northern hemisphere.

WHAT DO FOXES EAT?

Foxes kill and eat small creatures, including rats, mice and rabbits. In cities, foxes often feast on discarded food from rubbish bins and compost heaps.

WHAT DO GIANT PANDAS EAT?

The main food of the giant panda is bamboo. An adult panda eats up to 18 kilograms of bamboo leaves and stems a day.

WHAT DO GORILLAS EAT?

Gorillas eat plant food, such as leaves, buds, stems and fruit. Because their diet is juicy, gorillas rarely need to drink.

WHY DO TIGERS HAVE STRIPES?

Tigers cannot run fast for long distances. Their stripes help them hide among grasses and leaves so they can get close to their prey before pouncing.

WHY DO BEAVERS BUILD DAMS?

Beavers build their homes, or lodges, in streams or rivers. But first they need to build a dam to make an area of still water, or the current would wash the lodge away.

WHY DO RODENTS GET LONG IN THE TOOTH?

The two sharp teeth at the front of a rodent's jaw are the ones it uses for gnawing. These get worn down, but keep on growing throughout the rodent's life.

WHY DOES A CHAMELEON CHANGE COLOUR?

Changing colour helps a chameleon get near to its prey without being seen and allows it to hide from its enemies.

WHY DOES A KANGAROO HAVE A POUCH?

A kangaroo is only about 2 centimetres long when it is born. The female kangaroo has a pouch so that its young can complete its development in safety.

WHY DO SNAKES SHED THEIR SKIN?

Snakes shed their skin, or moult, to allow for growth and because their skin gets worn and damaged.

WHY ARE BIG EARS USEFUL?

Elephants live in hot climates, so they flap their ears to create a breeze. This breeze cools their surface blood vessels and the cooler blood is circulated to the rest of the elephant's body.

WHY DO ELEPHANTS HAVE TRUNKS?

An elephant's trunk is used to reach food from high in trees and for sucking up water to drink and to clean itself. The elephant can also smell with its trunk, pick up objects and caress its young.

WHY DOES A MONKEY HAVE A LONG TAIL?

To help it balance and control its movements as it leaps from branch to branch in the rainforest.

WHY DOES A RATTLESNAKE RATTLE?

Rattlesnakes make their rattling noise to warn their enemies to stay well away. The rattle is made by a number of hard rings of skin at the end of the tail.

CAN POLAR BEARS SWIM?

Polar bears swim well and spend long periods in the freezing Arctic water. They are well equipped to survive the cold. They have a dense layer of underfur as well as a thin layer of stiff, shiny outer coat. Under the skin is a thick layer of fat to give further protection.

CAN FLYING SQUIRRELS REALLY FLY?

No, but they can glide from tree to tree. When the flying squirrel leaps into the air, it stretches out the skin flaps at the sides of its body, which act like a parachute, enabling it to glide gently between branches.

CAN MONKEYS LIVE IN COLD PLACES?

Most monkeys are found in warm areas near to the equator, but some macaque monkeys live in cooler places. The rhesus macaque lives in the Himalayas as well as in parts of China and India, and the Japanese macaque survives freezing winters with the help of its thick coat.

CAN LIZARDS SWIM THROUGH SAND?

The sand skink is a unique kind of lizard that lives in the sandhills of the southeastern United States. It spends most of its time below the surface, pulling itself through the sand like a swimmer moves through water.

CAN HIPPOS SWIM?

The hippo spends most of its day in or near water and comes out onto land at night to feed on plants. It is a powerful swimmer and walks on the bottom of the river at surprisingly fast speeds.

HOW MANY SPECIES...

... OF BEAR?	Eight species, ranging in size from the sun bear to huge polar bears and brown bears.
... OF DOG AND FOX?	About 35 species, including 'true dogs' such as wolves, jackals and wild dogs.
... OF LIZARD?	Probably over 4,000 species. These belong to different groups, such as geckos, iguanas, skinks and chameleons.
... OF MONKEY?	About 260 species in two main groups. One group lives in Africa and Asia; the other lives in Central and South America.
... OF SNAKE?	About 2,700 species. They live on every continent except Antarctica.
... OF WILD CAT?	About 36 species, ranging from the tiger to the African wild cat, which is closely related to the domestic cat.

HOW MUCH DOES A KOALA EAT?

A koala eats about 500 grams of eucalyptus leaves every day, which it chews down to a fine pulp with its broad teeth.

HOW MUCH DO ELEPHANTS EAT?

A fully grown elephant eats 75 to 150 kilograms of plant food a day. Its diet includes grass, twigs, branches, leaves, flowers and fruits.

HOW BIG IS A BABY ELEPHANT?

A newborn baby African elephant weighs up to 120 kilograms and stands up to 1 metre high.

HOW LONG ARE AN ELEPHANT'S TUSKS?

The older an elephant is, the longer its tusks. One tusk in the British Museum measures 3.5 metres.

HOW BIG IS A BABY BEAR?

Bears have tiny babies. The polar bear gives birth to cubs of only about 1 kilogram, far smaller than most human babies.

HOW BIG IS A WOLF PACK?

In areas where there are plenty of large animals to catch, a pack may contain up to 30 wolves.

HOW FAST DO KANGAROOS MOVE?

A kangaroo bounds along on its strong back legs at up to 50 kilometres an hour. It can cover 13.5 metres in one giant bound.

HOW FAST DO SNAKES MOVE?

The fastest-moving snake on land is thought to be the black mamba, which lives in Africa. It can wriggle along at up to 11 kilometres an hour.

HOW TALL IS A GIRAFFE?

A male giraffe stands up to 5.5 metres tall to the tips of its horns.

WHICH IS THE BIGGEST...

... APE?

The gorilla. A fully grown male stands up to 1.7 metres tall and weighs as much as 220 kilograms.

... BEAR?

The polar bear is one of the largest bears. Fully grown males are up to 2.5 metres long.

... MONKEY?

The mandrill is the largest monkey, as it can grow to be 1 metre long. It lives in the tropical rainforests of Central Africa.

... CAT?

Tigers are the biggest of the big cats. They can measure over 3 metres long, including the tail, and weigh 250 kilograms or more.

... SNAKE?

The world's longest snake is the reticulated python, which grows to an amazing 10 metres long. The anaconda is heavier than the python but not quite as long.

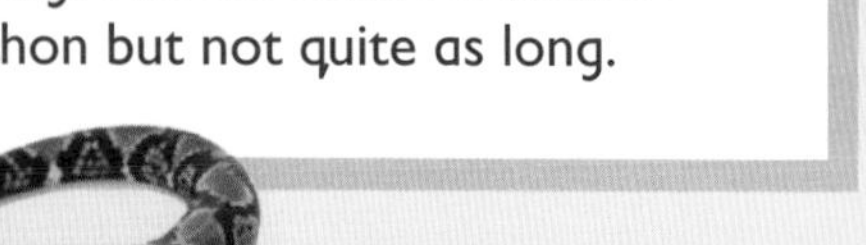

... RODENT?

The largest rodent in the world is the capybara. It measures up to 1.25 metres long and weighs up to 64 kilograms.

WHICH IS THE FASTEST CAT?

The cheetah. It has been timed running at 104 kilometres an hour over a distance of 200 metres – more than twice as fast as humans.

WHICH MONKEY MAKES THE LOUDEST NOISE?

Howler monkeys shout louder than other monkeys and are among the noisiest of all animals. Their voices carry for more than 3 kilometres.

WHICH IS THE LARGEST LIZARD?

The Komodo dragon, which lives on some Southeast Asian islands. It grows up to 3 metres long and hunts animals such as wild pigs and small deer.

WHICH IS THE MOST DANGEROUS SNAKE?

The saw-scaled carpet viper is probably the world's most dangerous snake. It is extremely aggressive and its poison can kill humans. Saw-scaled carpet vipers live in Africa and Asia.

WHEN IS A DOG REALLY A RAT?

A prairie dog is actually not a dog at all. It is a type of rodent, and lives in North America.

DO CHIMPS HUNT PREY?

Yes, they do. Although fruit is the main food of chimps, they also eat insects and hunt young animals, including monkeys.

IS A PLATYPUS A MARSUPIAL?

No. It is an unusual animal that lives in Australia. Unlike most mammals, which give birth to live young, the platypus lays eggs.

IS THE RHINO ENDANGERED?

All five species of rhinoceros are endangered. Rhinoceroses have been over-hunted for their horns, which are valuable in traditional medicine.

ARE RHINOCEROSES FIERCE?

White rhinos are usually peaceful, plant-eating animals. However, black rhinos can be ill-tempered and aggressive.

WHERE DO JAGUARS LIVE?

Jaguars live in the forests of Central and South America. They are good climbers and often clamber up trees to watch for prey.

IS THE GIANT PANDA REALLY A BEAR?

Genetic evidence suggests that the panda is a member of the bear family, not the raccoon family, as some experts previously thought.

IS A KOALA REALLY A BEAR?

No, it's a marsupial and not related to bears at all!

ARE THERE ANY POISONOUS LIZARDS?

There are only two poisonous lizards in the world, the Gila monster and the Mexican beaded lizard.

WHERE DO CHAMELEONS LIVE?

Most live in Africa and Madagascar. There are also a few Asian species and one kind that lives in parts of southern Europe.

ARE ALL SNAKES POISONOUS?

No. Only about a third of all snakes are poisonous and fewer still have poison strong enough to harm humans.

DO BEARS SLEEP THROUGH WINTER?

Yes. In the far north, food supplies are poor for much of the winter. Bears eat as much food as they can, then hide away in warm dens.

DO CHIMPANZEES USE TOOLS? Yes. The chimpanzee can get food by poking a stick into an ants' nest. It also uses stones to crack nuts and it makes sponges from chewed leaves to mop up water or wipe its body.

WHERE DO CHIMPANZEES LIVE?

Chimpanzees live in forests and grasslands in equatorial Africa. There is a less familiar chimpanzee species called the bonobo, which lives in rainforests in Congo in Africa.

WHERE DO ORANGUTANS LIVE?

Orangutans live in the rainforests of Sumatra and Borneo, in Southeast Asia. They sleep on the ground or in a nest of branches in the trees.

WHAT IS...

A MARINE MAMMAL?

Not all mammals live on land. Seals, sea lions and walruses are just some of the mammals that depend on the oceans for food. Marine mammals need to breathe air, so they have to come to the water's surface regularly. They have a thick layer of blubber, or fat, which keeps them warm in the water.

HOW FAST...

... DO FISH SWIM?	The sailfish can move at speeds of more than 110 kilometres an hour. Marlins and tunas are also fast swimmers.
... DO SHARKS SWIM?	Up to 80 kilometres an hour for short periods.
... DO SEA LIONS SWIM?	Up to 40 kilometres an hour.
... DO WHALES SWIM?	Blue whales can move at speeds of up to 30 kilometres an hour. Smaller whales, such as pilot whales and dolphins, may swim at more than 50 kilometres an hour.

HOW MANY...

...TYPES OF FROG AND TOAD?	There may be as many as 4,000 species. Most live in areas with plenty of rainfall.
...TYPES OF CROCODILE?	There are 14 species of crocodile, 2 species of alligator, several species of caiman and 1 species of gavial.
... KINDS OF SHARK?	Over 300 different species living all over the world. They range in size from dwarf dogfish to the giant whale shark.
... GROUPS OF WHALES?	There are two groups of whales: toothed whales and whales that catch food with baleen filters.

HOW BIG IS A BABY BLUE WHALE? A baby blue whale is about 8 metres long at birth and is the biggest baby in the animal kingdom.

HOW BIG IS A GREAT WHITE SHARK? Great white sharks are mostly about 7 metres long, but some can grow up to 12 metres.

HOW DOES A BLUE WHALE FEED? It opens its mouth and water full of krill flows in.

HOW DO TURTLES SWIM? Turtles 'fly' through the water with the help of their strong, paddle-shaped flippers. The water flows out at the sides of the mouth, leaving the krill behind on baleen – bristly plates in the whale's upper jaw. The whale then swallows.

1,700 kg

HOW BIG IS A WALRUS? The largest male walruses are more than 3 metres long and weigh 1,700 kilograms.

HOW CAN YOU TELL A CROCODILE FROM AN ALLIGATOR? A crocodile's teeth stick out when its mouth is shut!

HOW CAN YOU TELL A SEAL FROM A SEA LION? Sea lions have small ear flaps, whereas seals have only ear openings. Sea lions can bring their back flippers under the body to help them move on land, while seals drag themselves along.

WHY...

... DO SOME WHALES MIGRATE?

Whales such as humpbacks migrate – travel seasonally – to find the best conditions for feeding and breeding. They spend much of the year feeding in the waters of the Arctic and Antarctic, where there is lots of krill to eat. When it is time to give birth, the humpbacks travel to warmer waters near the equator.

... DOES A FLYING FISH 'FLY'?

A flying fish usually lifts itself above the water to escape from danger. It has extra-large fins, which act as 'wings'. After building up speed under the water, the fish lifts its fins and glides above the surface for a short distance.

... DO FROGS CROAK?

Male frogs make their croaking calls to attract females. The frog has a special sac of skin under its chin, which blows up and helps make the call louder.

WHICH IS THE BIGGEST SEAL? The male elephant seal is the biggest. It is 6.5 metres long and weighs up to 3,600 kilograms.

WHICH IS THE SMALLEST FROG? The smallest frog, and the smallest of all amphibians, is the Cuban frog, which measures around 9.8 millimetres long.

WHICH IS THE FIERCEST FRESHWATER FISH? The piranha with its sharp, flesh-ripping teeth, is the fiercest of all freshwater fish.

WHICH IS THE BIGGEST WHALE? The blue whale is the largest whale and also the largest mammal that has ever lived. It measures more than 30 metres long.

WHICH IS THE BIGGEST CROCODILE? The Nile crocodile grows up to 6 metres long, but the Indopacific crocodile, which lives in parts of Southeast Asia, may be even larger.

DO CROCODILES LAY EGGS? Yes. Most female crocodiles lay their eggs in a pit, then cover them with earth or sand, and guard them very carefully.

ARE BABY SEALS AND SEA LIONS BORN IN WATER?

No. Seals and sea lions come onto land to give birth and to feed their young.

WHERE DO SEA TURTLES LAY THEIR EGGS?

Female sea turtles dig a pit on a sandy beach in which to lay their eggs.

DO WHALES GIVE BIRTH IN WATER?

Yes. The baby whale comes out of the mother's body tail first. As soon as the head emerges, the mother and the other females help the baby swim to the surface to take its first breath.

WHAT DO SEA TURTLES EAT?

Most sea turtles eat a range of underwater creatures, such as clams, shrimp and snails.

DO ALL FROGS LAY THEIR EGGS IN WATER?

No, some frogs have very unusual breeding habits. The male marsupial frog carries his mate's eggs in a pouch on his back or hip.

WHAT DO CROCODILES EAT?

Baby crocodiles start by catching insects and spiders to eat. As they grow, fish and birds form a larger part of their diet. Fully grown crocodiles prey on anything that comes their way, even large animals such as giraffes.

WHAT IS...

... A CETACEAN?	Cetaceans are a group of marine mammals that includes whales, dolphins and porpoises. They are highly intelligent, have large tails and breathe air through the blowhole on the top of their head.
...A PORPOISE?	A porpoise is a small whale with a rounded head, not a beaked snout like a dolphin. They live in coastal waters in the Atlantic, Pacific and Indian Oceans.
...A NARWHAL?	A narwhal is a whale with a single long tusk at the front of its head. The tusk is actually a tooth, which grows out from the upper jaw.
... TUSKING?	'Tusking' is when two animals, such as male narwhals, rub their tusks together.
... SPYHOPPING?	Dolphins often 'spyhop', coming to the surface to look around.
...AN AMPHIBIAN?	Unlike other land animals, most amphibians lay their eggs in water. Young amphibians live and breathe in water, before transforming into air-breathing, land-living adults.
...A TADPOLE?	A tadpole is the young, or larva, of an amphibian such as a frog or newt. The amphibian egg is usually laid in water and hatches out into a small, swimming creature with a long tail.
... AN ANEMONEFISH?	Anemonefish live in sea anemones that thrive in tropical waters. They are the only fish that are immune to the poison in sea anemones.

ARE ALL SHARKS KILLERS?

No, two of the largest sharks, the whale shark and the basking shark, eat only tiny shrimp-like creatures.

ARE ELECTRIC EELS REALLY ELECTRIC?

Yes, they are. The electric eel's body contains special muscles that can release electrical charges into the water to stun its prey.

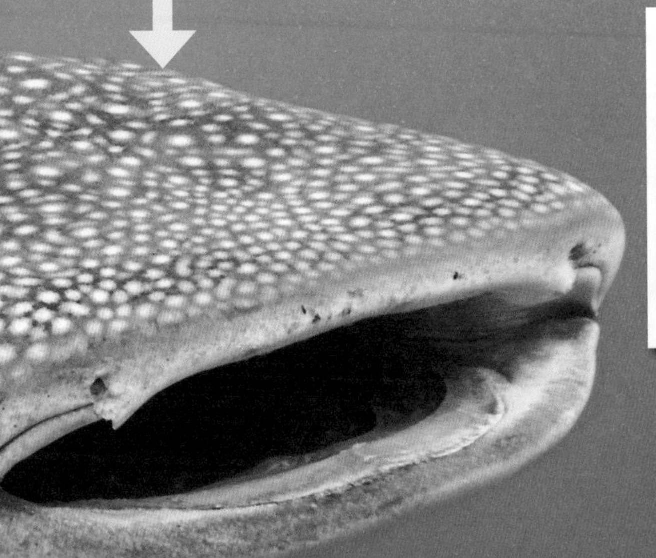

ARE CROCODILES AN ANCIENT SPECIES?

Crocodiles have looked the same since the time of the dinosaurs. They are 200 million years old.

ARE THERE ANY POISONOUS FISH IN THE SEA?

Yes. The puffer fish is one of the most poisonous. It has a powerful poison in some of its internal organs, which can kill a human.

ARE THERE SNAKES IN THE SEA?

Yes, there are 50 to 60 species of snake that spend their whole lives in the sea. They eat fish and other sea creatures and all are extremely poisonous.

DO ALL PENGUINS LIVE IN ANTARCTICA?

Most of the 18 species of penguin live in or near Antarctica, but some are found in warmer areas, such as around New Zealand. There are no penguins in the northern hemisphere.

DO VULTURES HUNT AND KILL PREY?

Vultures do not usually kill their prey. They are scavengers, feeding on animals that are already dead or have been killed by hunters such as lions. They have strong claws and beaks, and their bald head allows them to plunge into carcasses without matting their feathers.

DO EAGLES BUILD NESTS?

Yes, and the nest, called an eyrie, made by the bald eagle is the biggest made by any bird, at up to 5.5 metres deep. They are used again and again, with the eagles adding more nesting material each year.

HOW MANY...

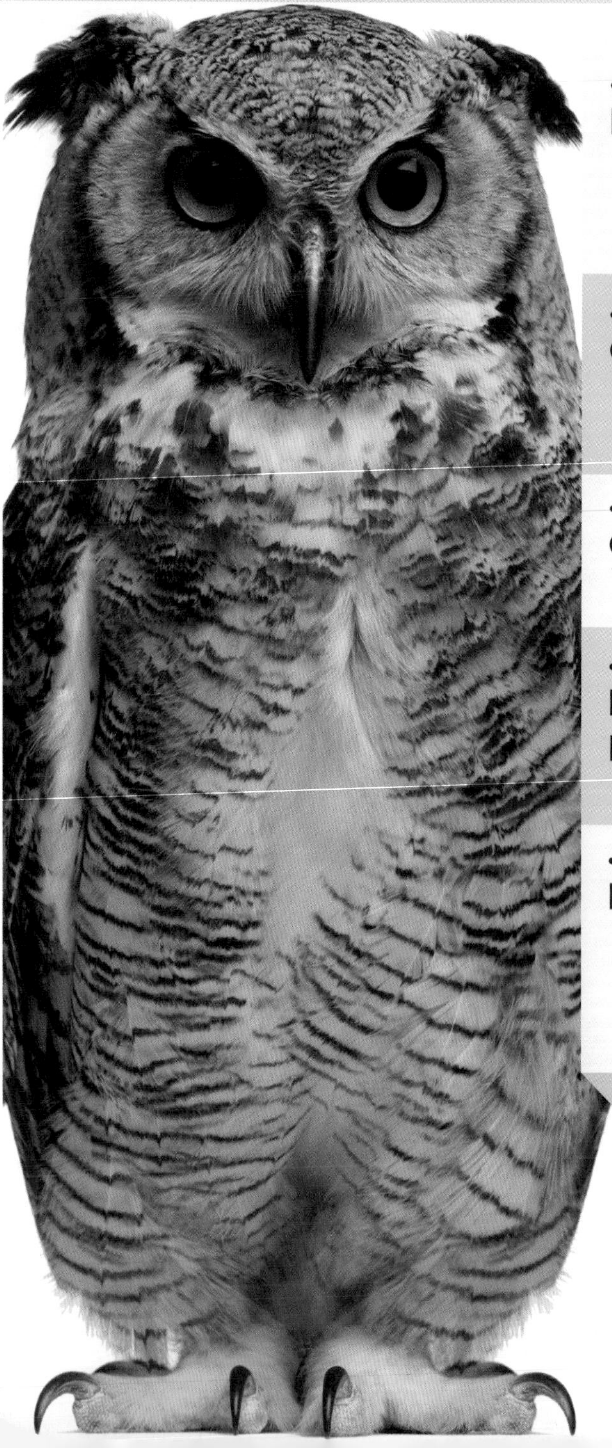

... SPECIES OF BIRD?	Around 10,000 different species. They inhabit every one of the world's ecosystems, from deserts to rainforests.
... KINDS OF GULL?	About 45. They live in all parts of the world, but there are more species north of the equator.
... KINDS OF OWL?	145 species. Owls are the only nocturnal birds of prey, usually hunting at night.
... KINDS OF BIRD OF PREY?	About 500 species, including eagles, hawks, buzzards, harriers, kites, falcons and vultures.
... SPECIES OF PARROT?	About 350 species, all of which live in the warmer regions of the world. Parrots are among the most intelligent birds.

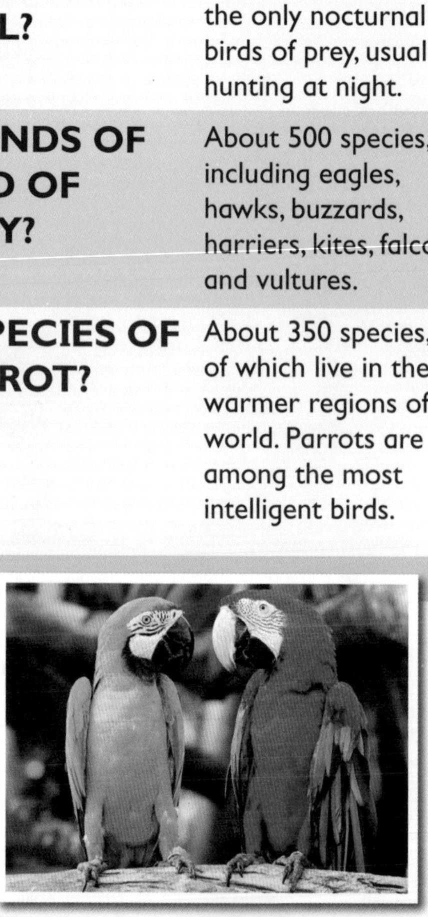

WHAT IS A GANNET?

Gannets are the largest seabirds in the North Atlantic Ocean, with a wingspan of up to 2 metres.

HOW DOES A GANNET CATCH ITS FOOD?

The gannet flies over the water looking for prey. When it sees something, it plunges into the ocean with its wings swept back, and seizes the catch in its beak.

WHAT IS A BIRD OF PREY? Birds of prey are hunters, feeding on small animals. They have keen eyesight, sharp hearing and strong beaks and claws.

HOW DO EAGLES KILL THEIR PREY? An eagle drops down onto its prey, seizes it in its long talons and crushes it to death.

WHY DOES A PELICAN HAVE A POUCH? The pelican has a pouch to help it catch fish. Water drains from the pouch, leaving any fish behind to be swallowed.

WHAT IS A TROPICBIRD?

A tropicbird is a seabird with two very long central tail feathers. There are three species, all of which fly over tropical oceans.

WHAT DOES AN OSPREY EAT? The osprey feeds mostly on fish. It dives to the water's surface and seizes fish in its feet.

HOW CAN OWLS HUNT AT NIGHT? Owls have excellent sight and very sharp hearing. Special soft-edged wing feathers enable them to beat their wings very quietly.

IS A PUFFIN A KIND OF PENGUIN? No, puffins belong to a family of birds called auks. They live in the northern hemisphere and are able to fly.

HOW FAST DO PENGUINS SWIM?

Penguins can swim at speeds of 13 kilometres an hour, but they may move even faster for short periods.

WHICH BIRD MAKES THE LONGEST JOURNEY?

The Arctic tern makes a round trip of 35,000 kilometres each year. The birds nest in the Arctic during the northern summer. To escape the northern winter, they travel south and spend the southern summer near Antarctica.

WHICH BIRD IS SCARLET?

The scarlet macaw is a parrot that lives in the forests of Central and South America.

WHICH IS THE BIGGEST PENGUIN?

The emperor penguin in Antarctica stands at about 115 centimetres tall. It is an expert swimmer and diver, using its wings as paddles.

WHICH BIRD HAS THE LONGEST WINGS?

The wandering albatross has the longest wings of any bird. When fully spread, they measure up to 3.3 metres.

WHICH IS THE SMALLEST PENGUIN?

The little, or fairy, penguin is only about 40 centimetres long. It lives in waters off the coasts of New Zealand and Tasmania, Australia.

WHICH IS THE BIGGEST BIRD OF PREY?

The Andean condor is the biggest bird of prey in the world. It measures up to 110 centimetres long and weighs up to 12 kilograms. Its huge wingspan is over 3 metres across.

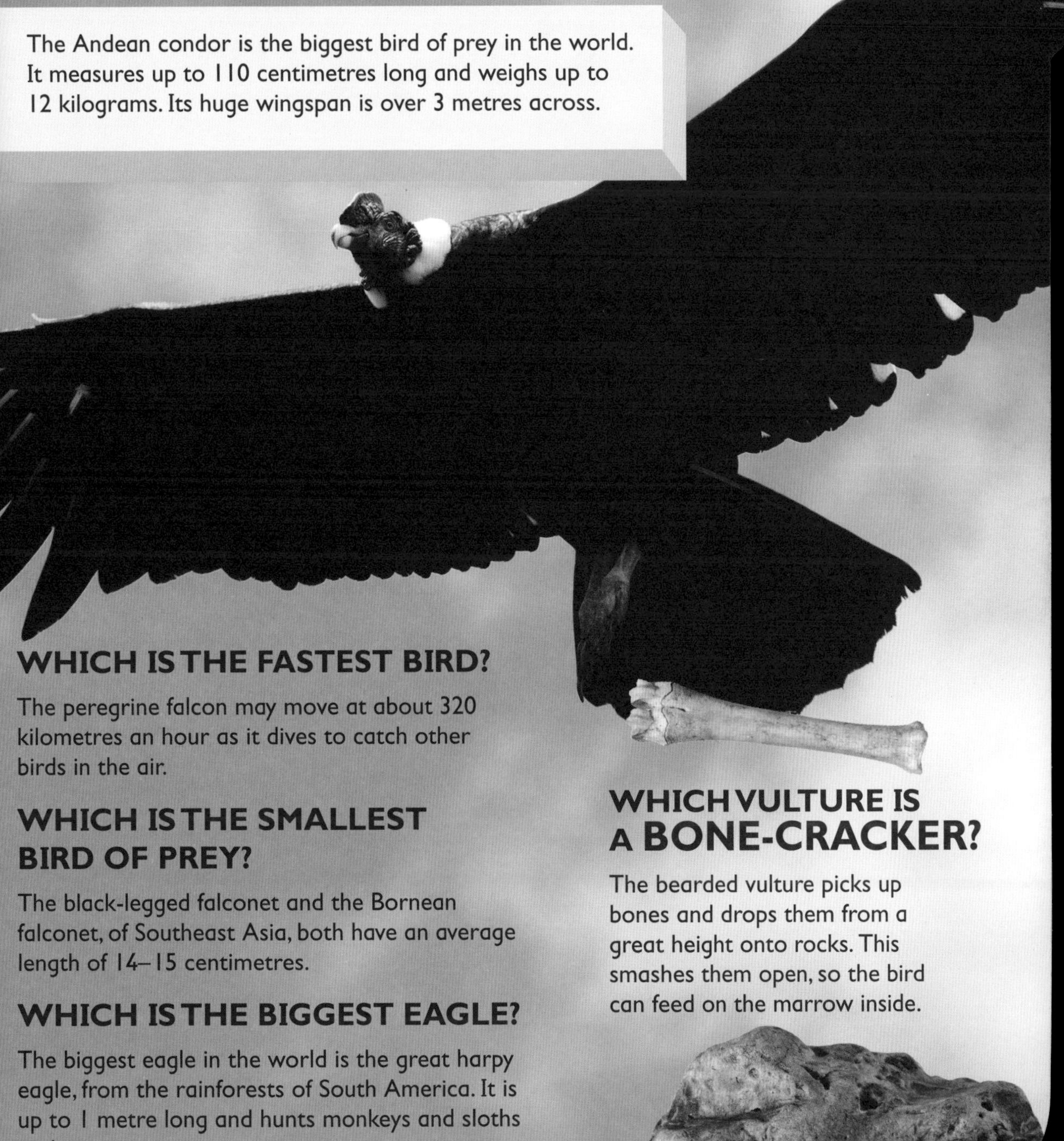

WHICH IS THE FASTEST BIRD?

The peregrine falcon may move at about 320 kilometres an hour as it dives to catch other birds in the air.

WHICH IS THE SMALLEST BIRD OF PREY?

The black-legged falconet and the Bornean falconet, of Southeast Asia, both have an average length of 14–15 centimetres.

WHICH IS THE BIGGEST EAGLE?

The biggest eagle in the world is the great harpy eagle, from the rainforests of South America. It is up to 1 metre long and hunts monkeys and sloths in the trees.

WHICH VULTURE IS A BONE-CRACKER?

The bearded vulture picks up bones and drops them from a great height onto rocks. This smashes them open, so the bird can feed on the marrow inside.

HOW MANY... KINDS OF PLANTS ARE THERE?

There are approximately 287,655 named species of plants, although many more are believed to exist. These range from trees, bushes and herbs to grasses, ferns and mosses. Most plants get their energy for growing from sunlight, using a process called photosynthesis.

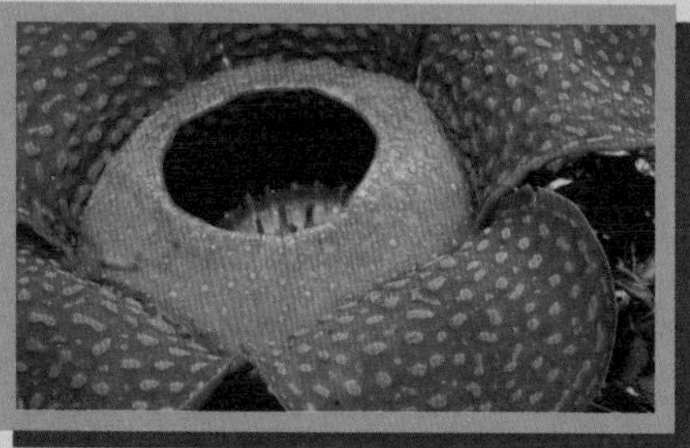

HOW DOES A FLOWER FORM SO QUICKLY?

The flower is already formed in miniature inside the bud, just waiting to open out.

WHY DO WE NEED PLANTS?

Plants reduce carbon dioxide and produce vital oxygen, which we need to survive.

HOW DO GREEN PLANTS FEED?

A pigment called chlorophyll helps to trap energy from the Sun. Plants use this energy to convert water and carbon dioxide into sugars and starch. This is called photosynthesis.

HOW DOES MISTLETOE FEED?

Mistletoe takes some nutrients from other plants by attaching itself to the branches of trees and shrubs.

HOW FAST DOES SAP FLOW THROUGH A TREE?

Sap is the fluid that transports water and food through plants. It may flow through a tree as fast as 1 metre every hour.

HOW MUCH SUGAR DO PLANTS MAKE IN A YEAR?

Scientists estimate that all the green plants in the world make more than 170 billion tonnes of sugar every year.

HOW DOES A VENUS FLY-TRAP CATCH ITS PREY?

It has a flattened, hinged pad at the end of each leaf, fringed with sensitive hairs. When an insect lands on the pad, the trap springs shut.

WHAT IS THE STINKIEST FLOWER?

The rafflesia in Southeast Asia mimics the aroma of rotting flesh to attract flies.

HOW DOES A PARASITIC PLANT FEED?

Parasitic plants grow into the tissues of another plant, called the host, and tap into its food and water transport system.

WHY ARE MOST PLANTS GREEN?

Because their stems and leaves contain the green pigment chlorophyll.

WHY DO SHOOTS GROW UPWARDS?

Most shoots grow upwards, towards sunlight. The growing tip of the shoot can detect the direction of the light.

WHAT MAKES A SEED GROW?

To grow, a seed needs moisture, warmth and air.

WHY DO ROOTS GROW DOWNWARDS?

Roots respond to gravity by releasing chemicals that prevent growth on the lower side, thus turning the root downwards.

HOW DO PLANTS TAKE IN WATER?

Plants use their roots to take in water from the ground. Water passes into the root across the cell walls of millions of tiny root hairs.

HOW DO PLANTS REPRODUCE?

Many plants reproduce by pollination. The pollen, containing the male cells, fertilizes the female ovules, which then produce seeds. The pollen can be taken to its destination by insects, birds, the wind or water.

HOW ARE FLOWERS POLLINATED?

The animal lands on the flower, gets showered with pollen, then moves to the next flower, transporting the pollen.

WHAT HAPPENS IN A FLOWER AFTER POLLINATION?

Pollen that has landed on the stigma of a flower sends a tube down into the ovary, which it enters to fertilize an ovule. Each ovule becomes a seed.

WHICH FLOWERS LAST FOR JUST ONE DAY?

The flowers of morning glory and daylilies open each morning and shrivel and die towards evening.

WHICH FLOWERS ARE POLLINATED BY MAMMALS?

The flowers of the African baobab tree are pollinated by bushbabies and bats.

HOW ARE SEEDS DISPERSED?

Birds eat berries and pass out the tougher seeds unharmed in their droppings. Some fruit capsules have hooks that catch in animal fur and are transported that way. Other seeds are carried by the wind.

CAN PLANTS REPRODUCE WITHOUT SEEDS?

Some plants spread by dispersing spores, which can produce a new plant without the need for pollination. Other plants send out runners or split off from bulbs, or swollen stems.

WHAT LIVES IN A TREE?

Insects, birds and wild bees may all choose to nest in a tree. Many mammals are also tree-dwellers, including squirrels, monkeys, sloths, bats and koalas.

WHAT IS THE NITROGEN CYCLE?

Bacteria in the soil use nitrogen from the air and turn it into a form that plants can use. Plants use the nitrogen to make proteins. Animals then eat the plants. Nitrogen returns to the soil in animal droppings, or when plant and animal bodies decay.

WHAT HAPPENS TO ALL THE LEAVES THAT FALL?

Dead leaves are attacked by fungi and bacteria, and break down, becoming part of the soil. The leaves are also eaten by animals, including worms and insects.

WHAT IS THE WORLD'S LONGEST SEAWEED?

Giant kelp is a huge seaweed that forms underwater forests in the coastal waters of California, USA. Its fronds can be up to 65 metres long, making it one of the tallest plants known.

WHICH PLANT GROWS THE SLOWEST?

The record for the slowest-growing plant probably goes to the dioon plant from Mexico. One specimen was recorded to have an average growth rate of 0.76 millimetres per year.

WHICH PLANT GROWS THE FASTEST?

The giant bamboo of Burma grows at up to 0.3 metres per day, making it one of the fastest growing of all plants.

HOW DEEP ARE THE DEEPEST ROOTS?

Roots of a South African fig were found to have penetrated 120 metres below the dry surface.

WHICH PLANT HAS THE LARGEST FLOATING LEAVES?

The giant waterlily of the Amazon region has huge leaves. They grow up to 2.65 metres across and can support the weight of a child.

HOW MANY PLANTS ARE USED AS FOOD?

About 12,000 species of plant are known to have been used by people as food.

WHICH PLANTS GIVE US OIL?

The olive plant, sunflower, corn (maize), soya bean, peanuts, oilseed rape, sesame and African oil palm.

WHAT PLANTS ARE USED TO MAKE SUGAR?

Sugar comes from the sugar cane, sugar beet and the sugar palm.

WHAT ARE THE MOST IMPORTANT FOOD CROPS?

Potatoes and cereals, such as wheat, rice and maize, form the basis of many people's diet.

WHAT IS BREADFRUIT?

Breadfruit is a tree native to the Malay archipelago. It has large edible fruits that are eaten as a vegetable.

WHERE WERE POTATOES FIRST GROWN?

In the Andes of South America, wild potatoes were first gathered as food by the native people.

WHICH FRUITS ARE GROWN FOR FOOD?

Fruits of the temperate regions include apples, pears and strawberries. In warmer regions, there are citrus fruits and other fruits such as papayas, pineapples and melons.

WHERE DID WHEAT COME FROM?

Wheat was probably first cultivated over 6,000 years ago in what is now Iraq.

WHAT IS WHEAT USED FOR?

Wheat is used to make flour for bread, biscuits, cakes, pasta, noodles and couscous.

HOW IS CHOCOLATE MADE?

The cacao tree develops fruits, called pods, on the sides of its trunk. Each pod contains 20 to 60 seeds – the cocoa 'beans'. The beans must be fermented, roasted and ground before they become cocoa powder, which is used to make chocolate.

WHAT DO PEOPLE DRINK THE MOST? After water, tea is the world's most consumed drink.

HOW IS TEA MADE? Tea comes from the leaves of a camellia grown in India, Sri Lanka, Indonesia, Japan and China. The young leaf tips are harvested, dried and crushed to make tea.

WHERE DOES COFFEE COME FROM?

Coffee comes from the berries of the coffee plant. Ripe berries are harvested, then dried. The hard stones inside are the coffee 'beans', which are then often roasted.

WHAT TREES GIVE US A SWEET, SUGARY SYRUP?

The sugar maple has a sweet sap, harvested to make maple syrup.

WHAT IS THE AMAZON COW-TREE?

The Amazon cow-tree is a tropical fig. It produces a milk-like sap, which can be drunk just like cow's milk.

WHAT TYPES OF THINGS CAN BE MADE FROM PLANTS?

Wood alone is used to make countless objects, big and small, from construction timbers to toys. All kinds of cloth are also made from plants – and so is the paper you are looking at!

WHAT ARE VIOLINS MADE OF?

The body of a violin is usually made from finely carved spruce and maple woods, creating its beautiful sound.

WHAT IS BALSA?

Balsa is the world's lightest timber. It is used for making models such as aeroplanes and also for rafts, life-belts and insulation.

HOW IS CORK PRODUCED?

Cork comes from a tree called the cork oak. The cork is the thick, spongy bark. It is stripped away from the lower trunk, then left to grow back for up to 10 years before the next harvest.

WHAT WOOD MAKES THE BEST CRICKET BAT?

The best bats are made in India, from the timber of the cricket-bat willow, a white willow.

WHAT IS KAPOK?

Kapok is similar to cotton. Fluffy seed fibres from the kapok tree are used to stuff mattresses, jackets, quilts and sleeping bags.

HOW IS COTTON TURNED INTO CLOTH?

Cotton is a soft fibre that grows naturally around the seeds of the cotton plant, forming 'bolls'. These are 'ginned' to remove the seeds; spun, or twisted, into thread; and then woven to make cloth.

HOW MANY THINGS CAN BE MADE FROM BAMBOO?

Bamboo is used for scaffolding and building houses, and for making paper, furniture, pipes, walking sticks, mats, hats, umbrellas, baskets, blinds, fans and brushes.

WHAT IS RUBBER?

Rubber is the sap of some plants, particularly the para rubber tree. The trees are pierced, or tapped, and the sap drips slowly into a waiting container.

CAN PLANTS PRODUCE FUEL TO RUN CARS?

The copaiba tree yields an oil similar to diesel that can be used to run engines. Oilseed rape, soya bean and the petroleum nut tree can also be used to produce biofuels, or plant fuels.

HOW...

... DO PLANTS RECYCLE WATER?

Plants return water to the air through transpiration. Water moves up through plants before evaporating from the stems and leaves.

... DO PLANTS MAKE SOIL MORE FERTILE?

When plants die, they decompose, releasing the chemicals in their tissues into the surrounding soil. This makes the soil more fertile.

... DO PLANTS HELP US RECLAIM LAND?

Some grasses can be planted on coastal dunes to stop sand from blowing away. Other plants tolerate toxic substances and gradually improve the quality of soil.

DO FORESTS HELP IMPROVE THE AIR?

Forests release huge quantities of water vapour and oxygen into the atmosphere. Plants also absorb carbon dioxide.

... ARE PLANTS USED TO CLEAN UP SEWAGE?

Sewage works use tiny algae and other microscopic organisms in their filter beds. These feed on pollutants and help to clean the water.

... CAN PLANTS BE USED TO HELP STOP EROSION?

Erosion is when soil is removed by natural forces such as wind and water. Plants can reduce this because their roots trap loose soil and stop it being blown or washed away.

HOW LONG HAVE PEOPLE BEEN USING PLANTS AS MEDICINE?

For at least 100,000 years. Today, scientists are still researching the valuable healing properties of plants for use in conventional medicines.

WHICH COUNTRIES USE THE MOST HERBAL REMEDIES?

In China and India, herbal remedies are used more than any other kind of medicine.

CAN PLANTS HELP FIGHT CANCER?

Several plants are effective against cancer tumours. Vincristine – an extract of the rosy periwinkle – is very effective against some types of leukaemia.

CAN WILLOWS HELP PAIN?

Willow twigs were once chewed to give pain relief. A compound similar to the drug aspirin was once extracted from willows and the herb meadowsweet.

WHICH PLANTS AID DIGESTION?

Many plants, including the herbs and spices used in cooking, help digestion. In Europe, the bitter extract of wild gentians provides a good remedy for digestive problems.

WHAT IS...

... GINSENG? Ginseng is related to ivy. It is claimed to help many conditions, including heart problems and headaches.

... JOJOBA? Jojoba is a bush found in Mexico. The fruits have an oily wax used in inks, body lotions and shampoo.

... QUININE? Quinine, from the bark of the quinine tree, can cure or prevent malaria.

... LUNGWORT? Lungwort is a herb with spotted leaves that are said to look like lungs. Some people use it to treat asthma.

WHAT IS... AN ECOSYSTEM?

An ecosystem is a community of plants and animals that live in the same area or environment. The world has many different ecosystems, each with its own climate, soil and living things. Some ecosystems are small, such as ponds or coral reefs. Other ecosystems, including forests and deserts, are much larger. Many ecosystems need to be protected because growing human populations are putting them under threat.

WHAT IS A DESERT?

A desert is an area that receives very little rain and so is unable to support much plant growth. Although many deserts are in hot regions, some of the world's deserts can be extremely cold.

WHICH IS THE HOTTEST DESERT?

Parts of the Sahara, in North Africa, and the Mojave Desert, in North America, experience extremely high temperatures. The average summer temperature may be over 40°C. In Death Valley in the Mojave Desert, temperatures of 57°C have been recorded.

WHICH IS THE BIGGEST DESERT?

The Sahara in North Africa covers an area of about 9,400,000 square kilometres. This is nearly as big as the United States of America.

HOW DOES A CACTUS SURVIVE IN THE DESERT?

Cacti generally store water in their stems. Most cacti are spiny, which probably protects them from being eaten by desert animals.

WHAT LIVES IN A LARGE CACTUS?

Holes in cactus stems provide nest sites for desert rodents and for birds like the tiny elf owl.

HOW DO DESERT FLOWERS SURVIVE?

Many desert flowers survive as seeds in the desert soil. When the next rains fall, they trigger the seeds to germinate.

HOW DO 'RESURRECTION' PLANTS SURVIVE?

In dry conditions, the leaves of these plants shrivel up and turn brown to cut down the loss of water. When it rains, they turn green again.

HOW DEEP DO THE ROOTS OF DESERT PLANTS GO?

Some have very long roots to tap into deep underground water sources. Mesquite roots often grow as deep as 20 metres.

HOW BIG IS THE LARGEST CACTUS?

A 125-year-old giant cactus, or saguaro, can measure up to 15 metres tall and weigh as much as 6 tonnes!

WHICH IS THE STRANGEST DESERT PLANT?

Welwitschia is probably the strangest. It lives for centuries, growing very slowly and producing just two twisted leathery leaves.

WHY ARE SOME DESERTS EXPANDING?

The Sahara grows larger each year, partly because the climate is getting gradually warmer, but mainly because the plant life on the edges of the desert has been destroyed by grazing animals.

WHICH IS THE DRIEST DESERT?

The Sahara is one of the driest deserts. The Atacama Desert in Chile is also very dry, with years often passing between rainfalls.

WHAT ARE LIVING STONES?

Living stones are desert plants from southern Africa. They grow low down on the desert's surface, looking like small pebbles or rocks.

WHAT IS...

...A RAIN SHADOW? A rain shadow is a dry region of land that lies close to a mountain range. The mountains block rain-bringing clouds, casting a 'shadow' of dryness.

...AN OASIS? An oasis is a place in the desert where water is in plentiful supply, such as at a pool fed by a spring.

...A JOSHUA TREE? The Joshua tree grows in the Mojave Desert, USA. Each of its leaves can survive for up to 20 years.

...A PRICKLY PEAR? It is a type of cactus. The fruits of prickly pears can be eaten, as long as their small spines are removed.

...A YUCCA PLANT? Yucca plants are succulents – they are adapted to very dry conditions and store water in their leaves.

WHAT IS GRASSLAND?

Grassland develops in temperate regions – lying between the polar areas and the tropics – that have warm summers and cold winters, and where there is not enough rainfall for trees and woods to grow.

WHAT NAMES ARE GIVEN TO GRASSLANDS?

The Asian grasslands are called the steppes, and the North American grasslands are the prairies. In Argentina they are called pampas, and in southern Africa the veld.

WHAT ARE GRASSLANDS USED FOR?

Because the soils are so fertile, much grassland has been ploughed and planted with crops. Grasslands are also used for grazing herds of animals, such as cows.

HOW DO GRASSLAND FIRES START?

Fires can start quite naturally, for example when lightning strikes dead or dying grass. In dry, windy weather, the sparks can quickly turn into a fire.

HOW DO GRASSLAND PLANTS SURVIVE FIRE?

Some survive fires by persisting as thickened roots, sprouting again after the fire has passed. Others germinate from seeds left behind in the soil.

WHAT IS WETLAND?

Wetlands include swamps, bogs and marshes. Wetland plants are adapted to living in water-soaked soil. Bulrushes, water lilies and mangroves are just some of the common wetland species.

HOW ARE WETLANDS DAMAGED?

When soil is drained, or too much water is pumped from the land nearby, wetlands suffer as the water table is lowered. They are also easily damaged by pollution: chemicals released from factories find their way into nearby streams.

WHAT FOOD PLANTS COME FROM WETLANDS?

The most important wetland crop is rice. It grows best in flooded fields called paddies.

WHY DO MOST WATER PLANTS GROW IN SHALLOW WATER?

Most plants need to root themselves in the soil, even if they live mainly submerged in the water. In deep water there is not enough sunlight for plants to grow successfully.

HOW DO WATER PLANTS GET THEIR FLOWERS POLLINATED?

Most water plants hold their flowers above the water, for pollination by the wind or by insects.

WHAT ARE CONIFEROUS FORESTS?

Coniferous forests contain coniferous trees such as pines and firs. These are evergreen trees, which do not lose their leaves in winter.

WHICH IS THE WORLD'S HIGHEST MOUNTAIN RANGE?

The Himalayas, in Asia. It contains 96 of the world's 109 peaks that are more than 7,315 metres above sea level.

HOW COLD IS MOUNTAIN AIR?

As you climb a mountain, the air temperature falls about 1°C for every 150 metres you ascend in height.

WHICH IS THE WORLD'S HIGHEST MOUNTAIN?

At 8,848 metres to the summit, Mount Everest, in the Himalayas, is the world's highest mountain.

WHAT IS THE TREE-LINE?

Trees cannot grow all the way up a mountain and the highest level for them is known as the tree-line.

WHY IS IT COLDER IN THE MOUNTAINS?

The Sun heats the ground and this heat is trapped by the Earth's atmosphere. As you go up a mountain, and rise above the zone in which the heat is held, the atmosphere becomes thinner and the air gets colder.

WHY IS IT DAMAGING TO CUT DOWN MOUNTAIN FORESTS?

Tree roots anchor the soil, preventing it being washed away by rain running down the slopes. Without trees, dangerous landslides can occur.

HOW DOES MOUNTAIN PLANT LIFE REFLECT HARSH CONDITIONS?

Conditions get harsher the higher you go up a mountain. Fir or pine forest on the upper slopes gives way to shrubs then grassland, followed by snow and rock.

WHY ARE ALPINE PLANTS POPULAR IN GARDENS?

Alpine plants are popular because they have bright flowers and tend to grow well in poor conditions.

WHY DO DIFFERENT PLANTS GROW ON DIFFERENT SIDES OF A MOUNTAIN?

Because on the south side (or north side in the southern hemisphere), there is more sunshine and conditions are warmer, while on the other side, the snow stays on the ground much longer.

HOW...

... DO PLANTS SURVIVE THE COLD?	Some grow close to the ground, keeping out of the wind. Others have thick, waxy or hairy leaves to help insulate them from the cold.
... DO PLANTS SURVIVE SNOW AND ICE?	Few plants can survive being frozen, but many thrive under snow. The snow acts like a blanket.
... DO MOUNTAIN PLANTS ATTRACT POLLINATORS?	Many mountain plants have large, colourful flowers to attract insects. Some track the Sun to warm their flowers, which encourages insects to sunbathe there.
... DO SOME MOUNTAIN PLANTS REPRODUCE WITHOUT FLOWERS?	Some grasses grow miniature plants where the flowers should be. These drop off and grow into new plants.
... DO PLANT-EATING ANIMALS FIND FOOD IN THE MOUNTAINS?	Many mountain mammals burrow under the snow and continue to feed on mountain plants. Others store fat in their bodies and hibernate during the winter.

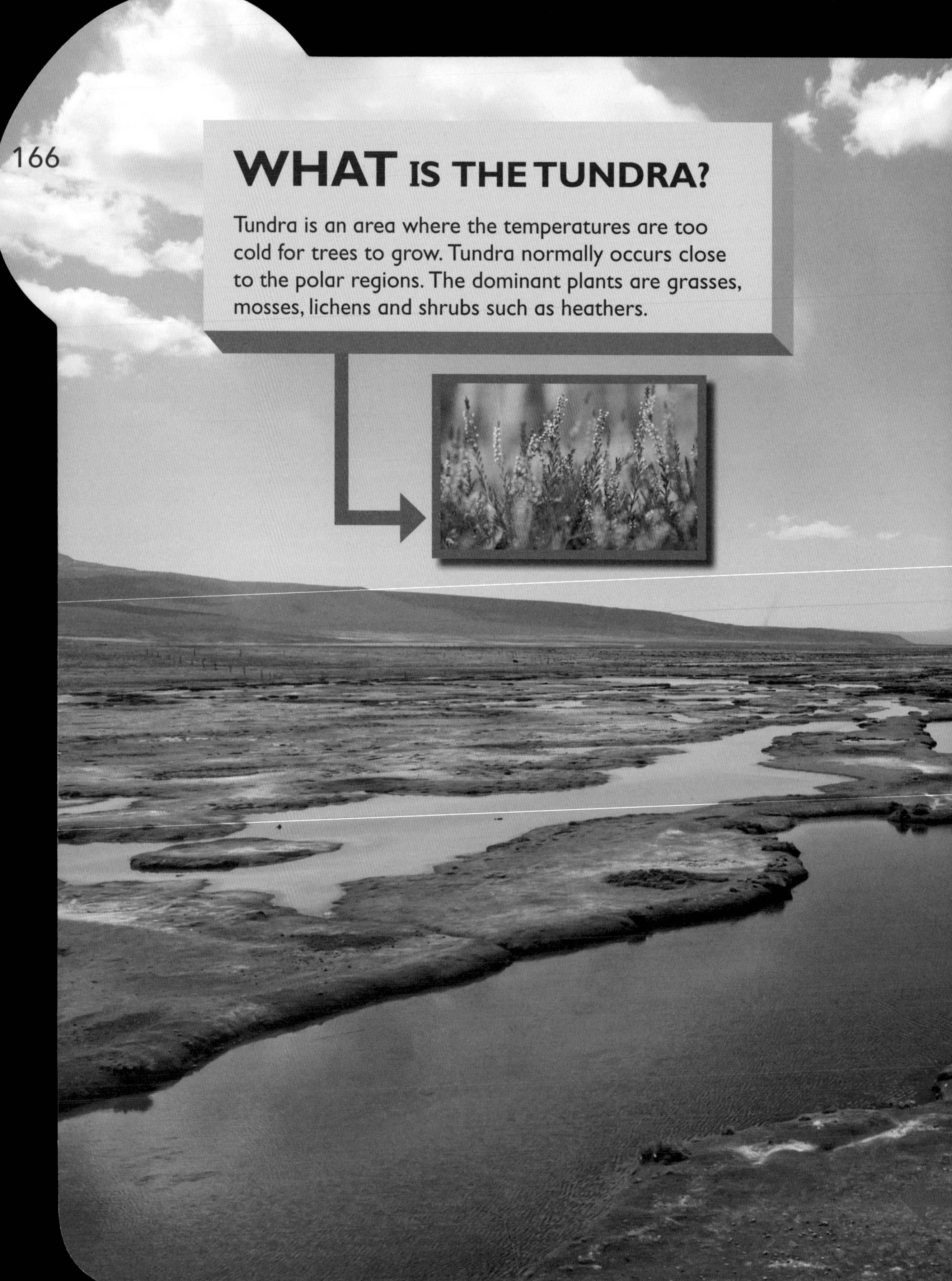

WHAT IS THE TUNDRA?

Tundra is an area where the temperatures are too cold for trees to grow. Tundra normally occurs close to the polar regions. The dominant plants are grasses, mosses, lichens and shrubs such as heathers.

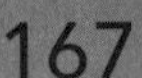

WHAT IS THE MOST NORTHERLY FLOWER?

The Arctic poppy has been found growing farther north than any other flower, at 83°N, or on a level with the north of Greenland.

WHERE IS THE TUNDRA?

Tundra lies north of the coniferous forest belt, in a band following the Arctic Circle. It covers about 25 million square kilometres, from Alaska, through Canada, Greenland, Iceland and Scandinavia into Siberia. Only a small area of the Antarctic has similar conditions, on the northern tip nearest South America.

WHERE ARE TEMPERATE FORESTS FOUND?

Temperate forests are found in parts of Europe, North America, eastern Asia, South America and Australasia.

ARE TEMPERATE FORESTS QUIETER IN WINTER?

Yes! Many of the birds migrate south in winter, while chirping forest insects hibernate or die.

WHY DO SOME TREES LOSE THEIR LEAVES IN THE AUTUMN?

Deciduous trees and other plants lose their leaves to shut down their main life processes and remain dormant until spring.

WHAT LIVES ON THE FOREST FLOOR?

Invertebrates such as beetles, woodlice, worms, slugs, snails and ants help break down dead leaves and roots, as well as providing food for mice and voles.

HOW ARE TEMPERATE FORESTS HARVESTED FOR WOOD?

Sometimes branches are cut from trees and the trees can then re-sprout from the base, to provide another crop of branches later. This is called coppicing.

WHAT ELSE DO WE GET FROM TEMPERATE FORESTS?

Charcoal is made by slowly burning certain kinds of wood. Many edible fungi grow in temperate woods, while woodland brambles and wild strawberries have edible fruits.

WHY DO MOST WOODLAND FLOWERS APPEAR IN SPRING?

By developing early, they can benefit from the sunlight before it is shut out by the trees. Insects, which help to pollinate flowers, may also find it easier to spot them before the rest of the vegetation grows.

WHICH FOREST TREE CAN BE TRACKED DOWN BY ITS SOUND?

The leaves of the aspen tree move from side to side in the wind and rustle against each other, even in the lightest breeze.

WHICH ARE THE MOST COMMON TREES?

The most common trees in deciduous forests are oaks, beeches, maples and birches. Common coniferous trees are pines, firs and spruces.

HOW OLD CAN FOREST TREES GET?

Many forest trees reach a great age, notably oaks, which live between 200 and 400 years. Most elms live to about 150 years.

WHERE ARE THE RAINFORESTS?

The world's largest rainforest is around Brazil's Amazon River and the foothills of the Andes Mountains. The world's main areas of tropical rainforest are in South and Central America, West and Central Africa, Southeast Asia and north Australia.

WHY DO WE NEED RAINFORESTS?

Rainforests help preserve the planet's atmosphere by releasing huge quantities of water vapour and oxygen, and absorbing carbon dioxide.

WHAT DO WE GET FROM RAINFORESTS?

We get many things from rainforests, including timber, Brazil nuts, fruit, rubber, rattan, cosmetics and medicines.

HOW FAST ARE RAINFORESTS BEING DESTROYED?

Every year an area of rainforest the size of the American state of Wisconsin is lost.

HOW MUCH RAIN FALLS IN THE RAINFOREST?

In many tropical rainforests, the rainfall is more than 2 metres per year.

ARE RAINFORESTS VITAL?

Yes! Rainforests are home to two-thirds of the world's animal and plant species. And without rainforests to regulate the Earth's atmosphere, climate change would speed up.

WHY ARE RAINFORESTS BEING CUT DOWN?

Many rainforests are destroyed so the land can be used for crops, or for grazing. Tropical forest soils are fertile and many crops can be grown after the trees have been felled.

HOW MANY LAYERS MAKE UP A RAINFOREST?

The rainforest is in four basic layers. At the top are the very tallest trees. Below is the canopy, a dense cover of foliage. The understorey is a layer of shrubs, while the forest floor below is relatively bare.

HOW TALL ARE THE BIGGEST RAINFOREST TREES?

The main canopy of the rainforest develops at around 30 metres, with occasional taller trees rising to 50 metres or more.

WHAT STOPS THE TALL TREES FROM BEING BLOWN OVER?

Many of the taller forest trees have special supporting flanges near the base of their trunks, called stilts or buttresses.

HOW MANY DIFFERENT KINDS OF TREES ARE IN A RAINFOREST?

Just one hectare of tropical rainforest can contain 600 species of trees.

WHAT IS AN AIR-PLANT?

An air-plant grows without anchoring itself to the ground. It gets the moisture it needs direct from the damp air.

WHAT ARE LIANES?

Lianes, or lianas, are plants that clamber over and dangle from rainforest trees.

WHAT'S A STRANGLER FIG?

The strangler starts out as a seed high in a tree. The seedling sends long roots to the ground, then starts to surround the host tree, slowly suffocating it.

WHICH PLANTS TRAP RAIN WATER?

Bromeliads have special leaves that form a waterproof cup to catch rain water before it reaches the ground.

HOW DO WE...

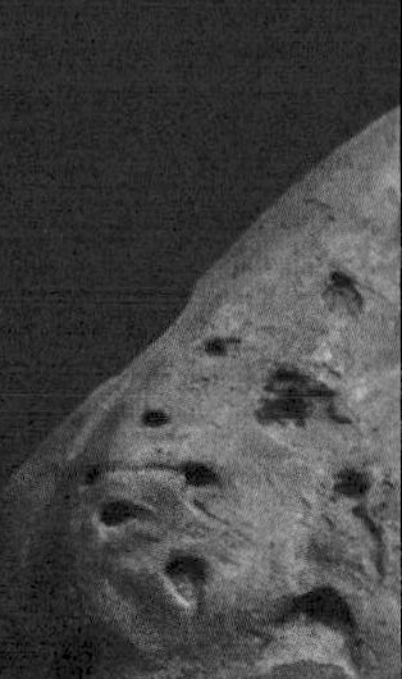

HOW IS THE EARTH'S HISTORY DIVIDED?

Scientists divide the last 590 million years into three eras: the Paleozoic (meaning old life), Mesozoic (middle life) and Cenozoic (new life). Earth's history before the Paleozoic era is divided into three eons: the Hadean, Archean and Proterozoic.

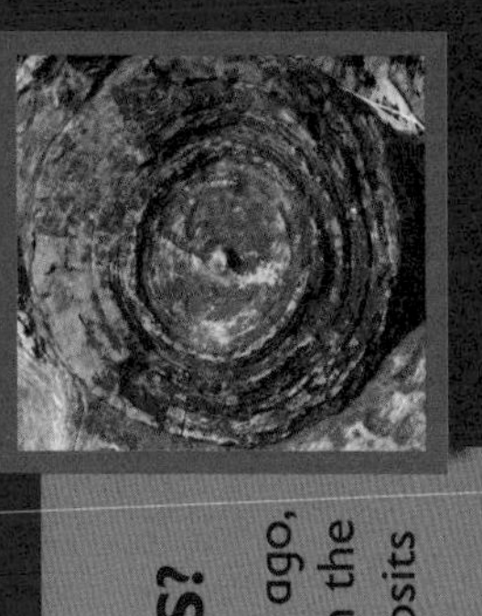

WHAT ARE STROMATOLITES?

About 3,800 million years ago, primitive life forms lived in the oceans. They formed deposits called stromatolites.

WHY WASN'T THERE LIFE ON EARTH STRAIGHT AWAY?

Life did not exist for the first 400–800 million years because the Earth's surface was probably molten.

WHAT DID EARLY ANIMALS LOOK LIKE?

By around 500 million years ago, bacteria in the oceans had evolved into the earliest fish with funnel-like sucking mouths.

WHY IS THE CAMBRIAN PERIOD IMPORTANT?

Before the Cambrian period, most living creatures were soft-bodied and left few fossils. During the Cambrian period, many creatures had hard parts, which were preserved as fossils in layers of rock.

WHAT WERE THE FIRST ANIMALS WITH BACKBONES?

Jawless fish were the first animals with backbones. They appeared during the Ordovician period.

WHEN DID PLANTS START TO GROW ON LAND?

The first land plants appeared in the Silurian period. Plants produced oxygen and provided food for the first land animals.

3,500 MILLION YEARS BC

500 MILLION YEARS BC

WHAT IS EVOLUTION?

Evolution is the process of how life forms change over the course of generations. When an animal develops a successful new feature, it is passed down to future generations.

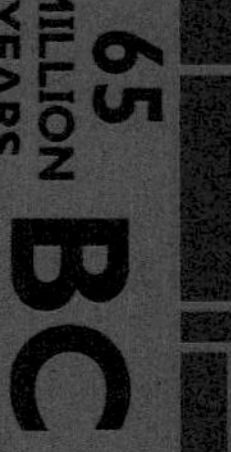

WHAT ARE PERIODS AND EPOCHS?

The geological eras are subdivided into periods. Periods are then divided into epochs.

WHAT WERE THE FIRST LAND ANIMALS?

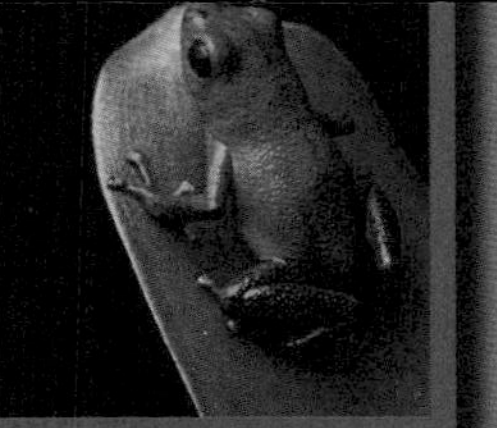

Amphibians. They first developed in the Devonian period from fish whose fins had evolved into limbs.

WHY DID DINOSAURS BECOME EXTINCT?

Many experts believe an enormous asteroid struck the Earth. The impact threw up a huge cloud of dust, which blocked sunlight for a long time. Land plants died and the dinosaurs starved to death.

WHEN DID MAMMALS FIRST APPEAR?

Mammals lived on Earth from at least the start of the Jurassic period. But they did not become common until after the extinction of the dinosaurs.

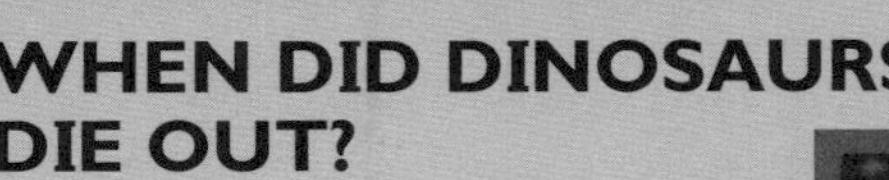

WHEN DID DINOSAURS DIE OUT?

At the end of the Cretaceous period, 65 million years ago.

WHEN DID PEOPLE FIRST LIVE ON EARTH?

Hominids (ape-like creatures that walked upright) first appeared on Earth over 4 million years ago.

24,000 YEARS BC

WHO WERE THE NEANDERTHALS?

Neanderthals were relatives of modern humans that disappeared 24,000 years ago.

WHAT ARE FOSSILS?

Fossils are the impressions of ancient life preserved in rocks. When creatures die, their remains are often slowly buried in sand or soil. Their soft parts usually rot, but the hard parts – such as bones, teeth and shells – can be preserved as minerals or moulds in the rock.

WHAT ARE TRACE FOSSILS?

Trace fossils give information about animals that lived in ancient times. Examples include animal burrows and footprints.

HOW ARE FOOTPRINTS PRESERVED?

Footprints can be preserved when the mud in which they are made quickly hardens and then is buried under more mud.

WHAT CAN SCIENTISTS LEARN FROM DINOSAUR FOOTPRINTS?

Dinosaur tracks can tell scientists about the length of the animal's legs and the speed at which it was moving.

HOW ARE FOSSILS TURNED TO STONE?

When tree trunks or bones are buried, minerals deposited from water sometimes replace the original material. The wood or bone is then petrified, or turned to stone.

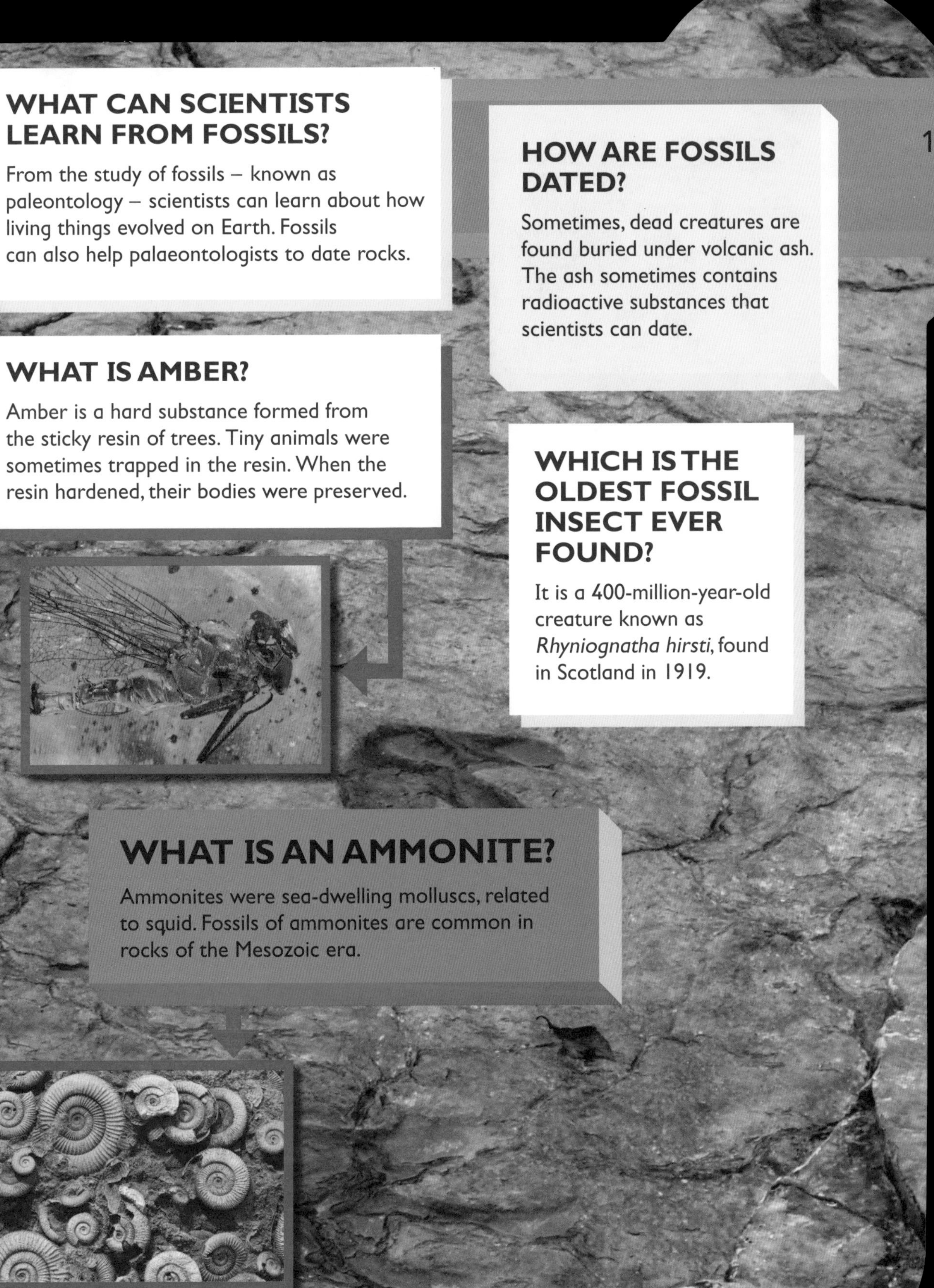

WHAT CAN SCIENTISTS LEARN FROM FOSSILS?

From the study of fossils – known as paleontology – scientists can learn about how living things evolved on Earth. Fossils can also help palaeontologists to date rocks.

WHAT IS AMBER?

Amber is a hard substance formed from the sticky resin of trees. Tiny animals were sometimes trapped in the resin. When the resin hardened, their bodies were preserved.

WHAT IS AN AMMONITE?

Ammonites were sea-dwelling molluscs, related to squid. Fossils of ammonites are common in rocks of the Mesozoic era.

HOW ARE FOSSILS DATED?

Sometimes, dead creatures are found buried under volcanic ash. The ash sometimes contains radioactive substances that scientists can date.

WHICH IS THE OLDEST FOSSIL INSECT EVER FOUND?

It is a 400-million-year-old creature known as *Rhyniognatha hirsti*, found in Scotland in 1919.

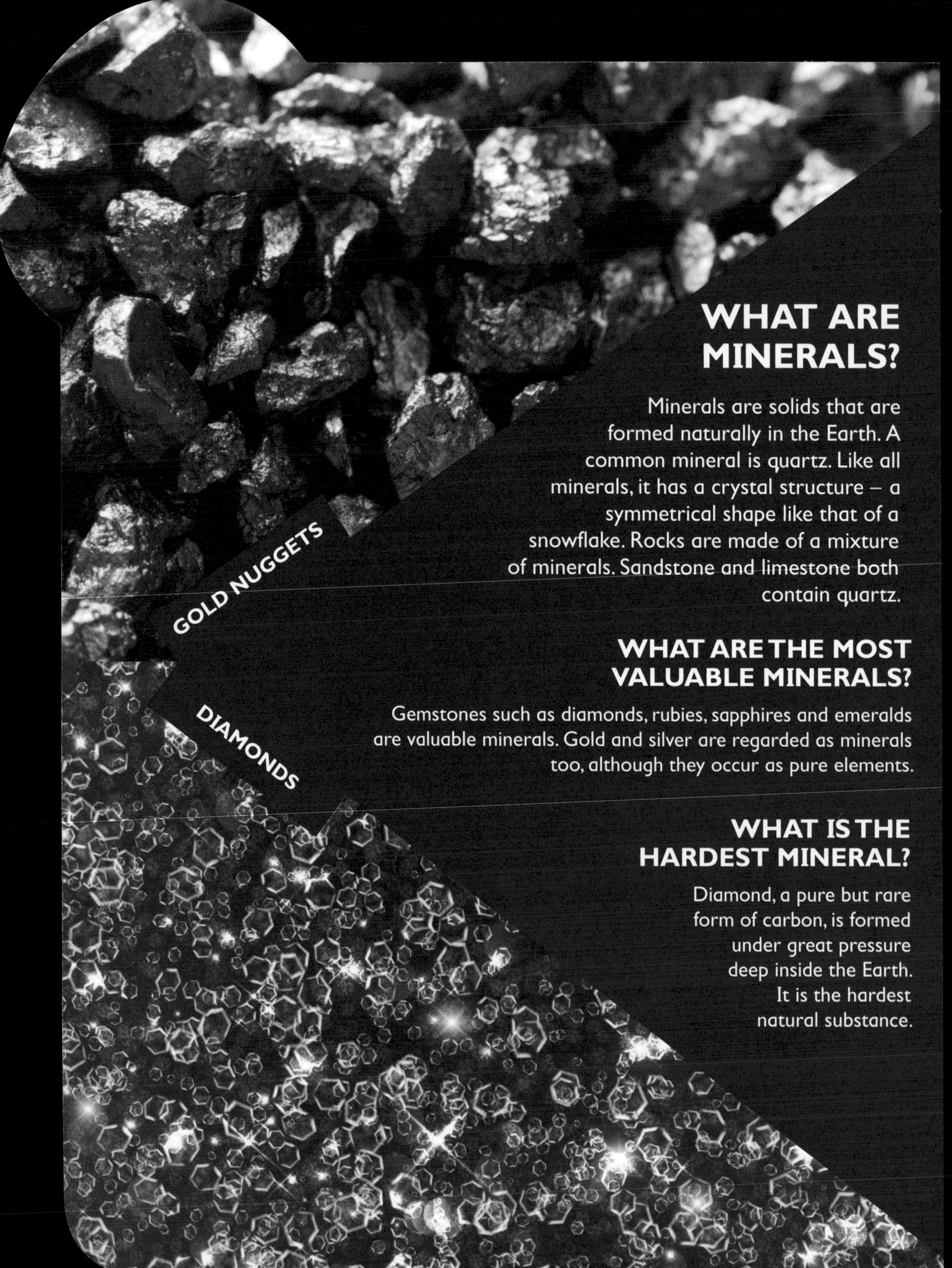

WHAT ARE MINERALS?

Minerals are solids that are formed naturally in the Earth. A common mineral is quartz. Like all minerals, it has a crystal structure – a symmetrical shape like that of a snowflake. Rocks are made of a mixture of minerals. Sandstone and limestone both contain quartz.

WHAT ARE THE MOST VALUABLE MINERALS?

Gemstones such as diamonds, rubies, sapphires and emeralds are valuable minerals. Gold and silver are regarded as minerals too, although they occur as pure elements.

WHAT IS THE HARDEST MINERAL?

Diamond, a pure but rare form of carbon, is formed under great pressure deep inside the Earth. It is the hardest natural substance.

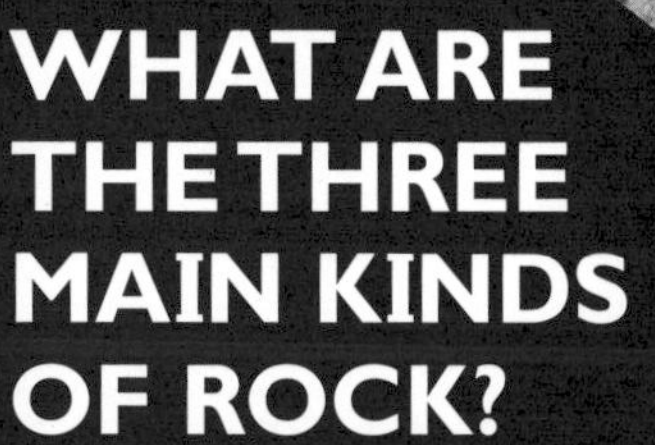

WHAT ARE THE THREE MAIN KINDS OF ROCK?

There are igneous, sedimentary and metamorphic rocks. Igneous rocks, such as basalt and granites, are formed from cooled magma. Many sedimentary rocks are made from worn fragments of other rocks. For example, sandstone is formed from sand. Sand consists mainly of quartz, a mineral found in granite. Metamorphic rocks are changed by heat and pressure. For example, great heat turns limestone into marble.

GRANITE

MARBLE

WHAT COMMON ROCKS ARE USED FOR BUILDINGS?

Two sedimentary rocks, limestone and sandstone, and the igneous rock granite are all good building stones. The metamorphic rock marble is often used to decorate buildings.

WHAT IS THE EARTH'S SURFACE MADE FROM?

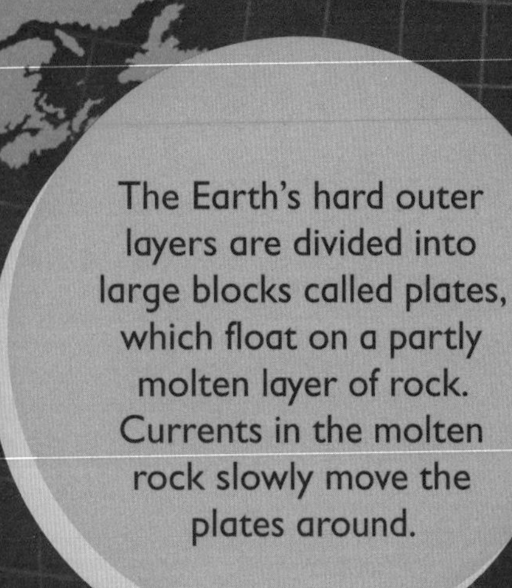

The Earth's hard outer layers are divided into large blocks called plates, which float on a partly molten layer of rock. Currents in the molten rock slowly move the plates around.

HOW MANY PLATES COVER THE EARTH?

There are seven major and seven minor plates.

WHAT HAPPENS WHEN PLATES COLLIDE?

If plates collide beneath an ocean, one plate is pulled beneath the other and is melted and recycled. On land, when continents collide, their edges are squeezed up into new mountain ranges.

HOW FAST DO PLATES MOVE? Plates move, on average, between 4 and 7 centimetres a year.

CAN PLATES MOVE SIDEWAYS?

Yes. Plates can move apart, push against each other or move sideways along huge cracks in the ground.

HOW DEEP ARE PLATES? Their exact thickness is uncertain but the larger plates could be up to 145 kilometres in places.

WHEN DID THE HIMALAYAS FORM? They started to form when plates collided about 50 million years ago.

WHAT IS THE EARTH'S MANTLE? The mantle is a partly molten rocky shell that surrounds the Earth's core and makes up 70% of the Earth's volume.

HAS EARTH ALWAYS LOOKED THE SAME?

No. If aliens had visited Earth 200 million years ago, they would have seen one huge continent surrounded by one ocean.

220 million years ago

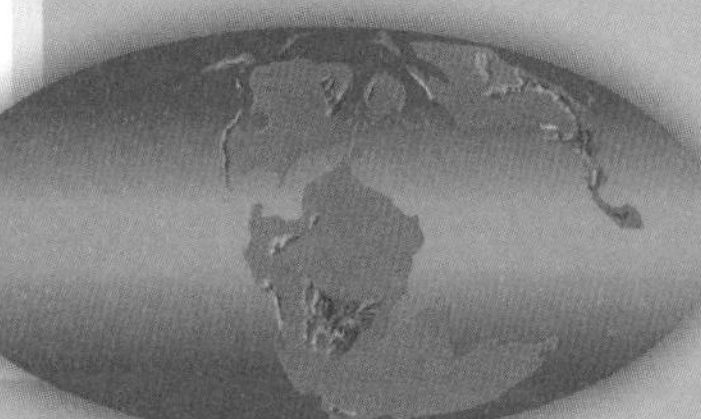

155 million years ago

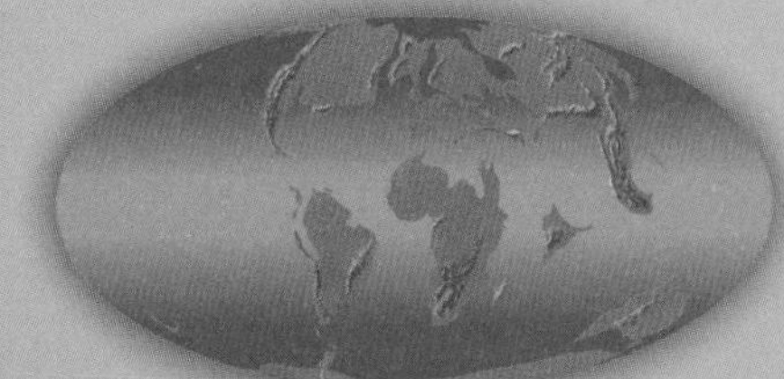

60 million years ago

WHAT IS CONTINENTAL DRIFT?
The continents lie on different plates, which constantly move. This movement is called continental drift.

HOW IS CONTINENTAL DRIFT MEASURED?
Around the world, observation stations measure the time taken for lasers to bounce back from satellites. This provides details of where the continents are and how they are moving.

ARE THE CONTINENTS STILL MOVING?
Yes. Africa is moving northwards into Europe at the rate of a few millimetres a year. The Americas are moving farther from Africa.

WHO FIRST SUGGESTED THE IDEA OF CONTINENTAL DRIFT?
F.B. Taylor and Alfred Wegener both suggested the idea in the early 1900s.

HAVE FOSSILS HELPED TO PROVE CONTINENTAL DRIFT? Fossils of animals that could not have swam across oceans have been found in different continents. This suggests that animals could once walk from one continent to another.

HOW WAS HAWAII FORMED?

The Hawaiian islands were created as the Pacific Plate passed over a hot spot in the mantle. A series of new volcanoes was punched up through the surface. Each of the Hawaiian islands has a volcano.

WHAT MAKES A VOLCANO ERUPT?

Volcanoes erupt when hot molten rock – or magma – from deep down in the Earth's mantle rises through the Earth's hard outer layers. When it reaches the Earth's surface, the magma is called lava.

WHAT IS AN EXTINCT VOLCANO?

Volcanoes that have not erupted in recorded history are said to be 'extinct'. This means that scientists consider they will not erupt again.

WHAT ARE HOT SPOTS?

Some volcanoes lie far from plate edges. They form over 'hot spots' – areas of great heat in the Earth's mantle. Hawaii in the Pacific Ocean is over a hot spot.

DO VOLCANOES DO ANY GOOD?

Volcanic eruptions cause tremendous damage, but soil formed from volcanic ash is extremely fertile. Volcanic rocks are also used in building and chemical industries.

WHAT IS A DORMANT VOLCANO?

Some active volcanoes erupt only now and then. When they are not erupting, they are said to be dormant, or sleeping.

DO EARTHQUAKES AND VOLCANOES OCCUR IN THE SAME PLACES?

Yes, most active volcanoes occur near the edges of moving plates. Earthquakes are common in these regions too.

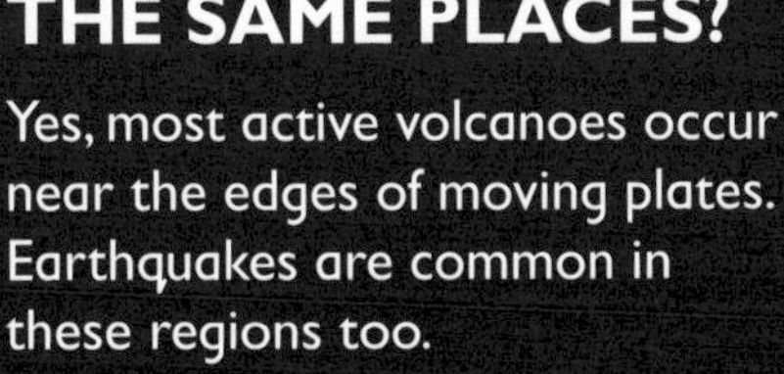

WHAT CAUSES AN EARTHQUAKE?

The edges of the Earth's plates are jammed together. Gradually, currents under the plates build up, increasing pressure, and the plates move in a jerk. This shakes all the rocks around them, setting off an earthquake.

WHAT IS A TSUNAMI?

Earthquakes on the seabed trigger waves called tsunamis. Tsunamis travel through the water at up to 800 kilometres an hour, creating deadly waves many metres high.

CAN SCIENTISTS PREDICT EARTHQUAKES?

In 1975, Chinese scientists correctly predicted an earthquake using a seismograph to measure plate movements. But scientists have not yet found an absolutely certain way of forecasting earthquakes.

WHAT ARE HOT SPRINGS AND GEYSERS?

These are places where underground water, heated by magma inside the Earth, breaks through to the surface. Warm water bubbles up at hot springs. Geysers hurl boiling water and steam into the air.

HOW BIG IS...

... ASIA?	44,580,000 sq km
... AFRICA?	30,220,000 sq km
... NORTH AMERICA?	24,710,000 sq km
... SOUTH AMERICA?	17,840,000 sq km
... ANTARCTICA?	14,000,000 sq km
... EUROPE?	10,180,000 sq km
... AUSTRALIA?	7,741,000 sq km

WHICH IS THE...

...TALLEST VOLCANO?	Mauna Kea in Hawaii.
... LONGEST RIVER?	The Nile in northeast Africa, at 6,617 kilometres long.
... DEEPEST LAKE?	Lake Baikal, in Siberia, eastern Russia.
... LOWEST POINT ON LAND?	The shoreline of the Dead Sea, at 400 metres below sea level.
... DEEPEST CAVE?	The Krubera cave, in Georgia. It is more than 2,000 metres deep.

WHICH IS THE LARGEST...

... OCEAN?	The Pacific, at 165 million sq km
... ISLAND?	Greenland, at 2,166,000 sq km
... LAKE?	Lake Superior, at 82,100 sq km

WHAT IS...

WEATHERING?

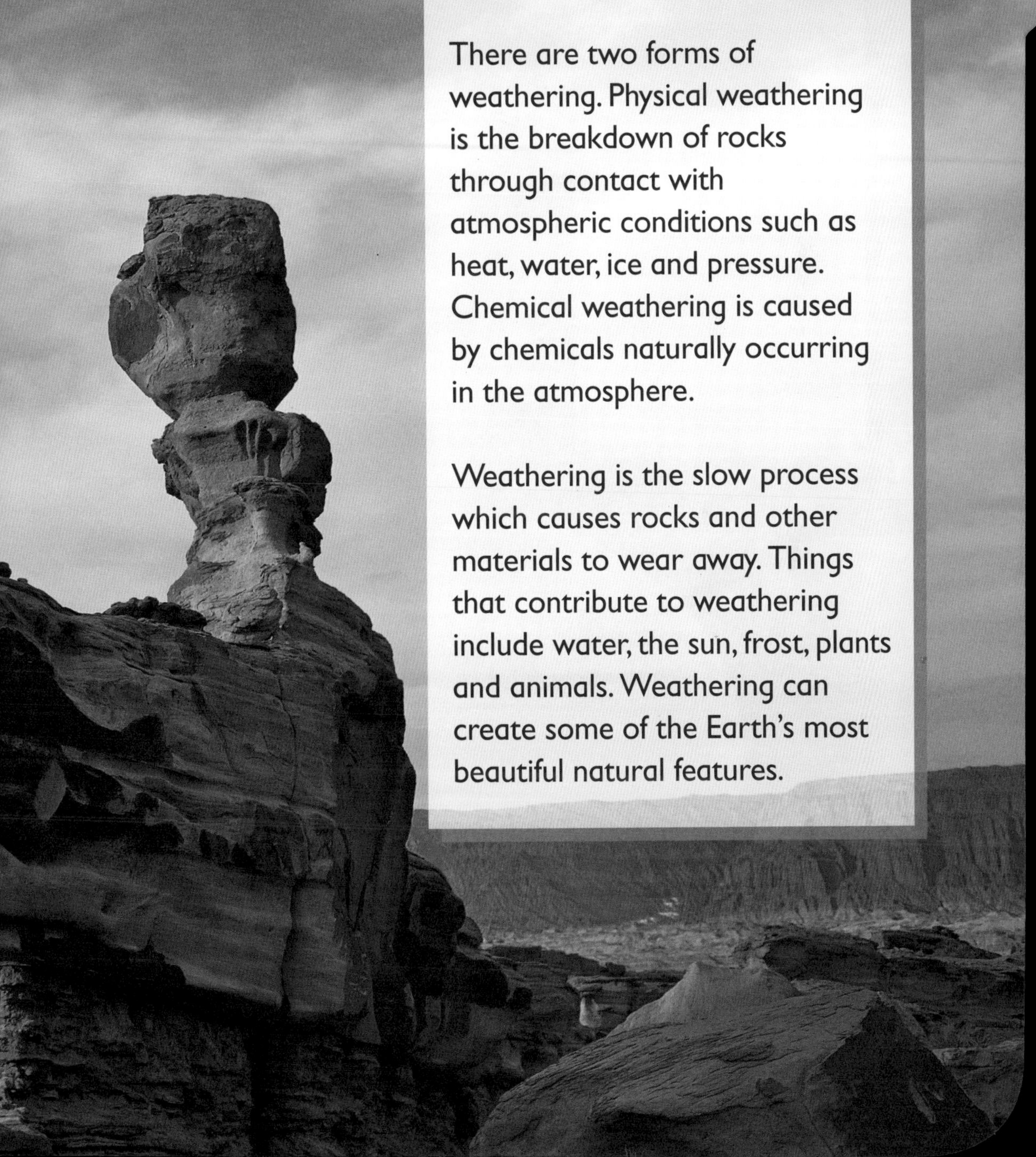

There are two forms of weathering. Physical weathering is the breakdown of rocks through contact with atmospheric conditions such as heat, water, ice and pressure. Chemical weathering is caused by chemicals naturally occurring in the atmosphere.

Weathering is the slow process which causes rocks and other materials to wear away. Things that contribute to weathering include water, the sun, frost, plants and animals. Weathering can create some of the Earth's most beautiful natural features.

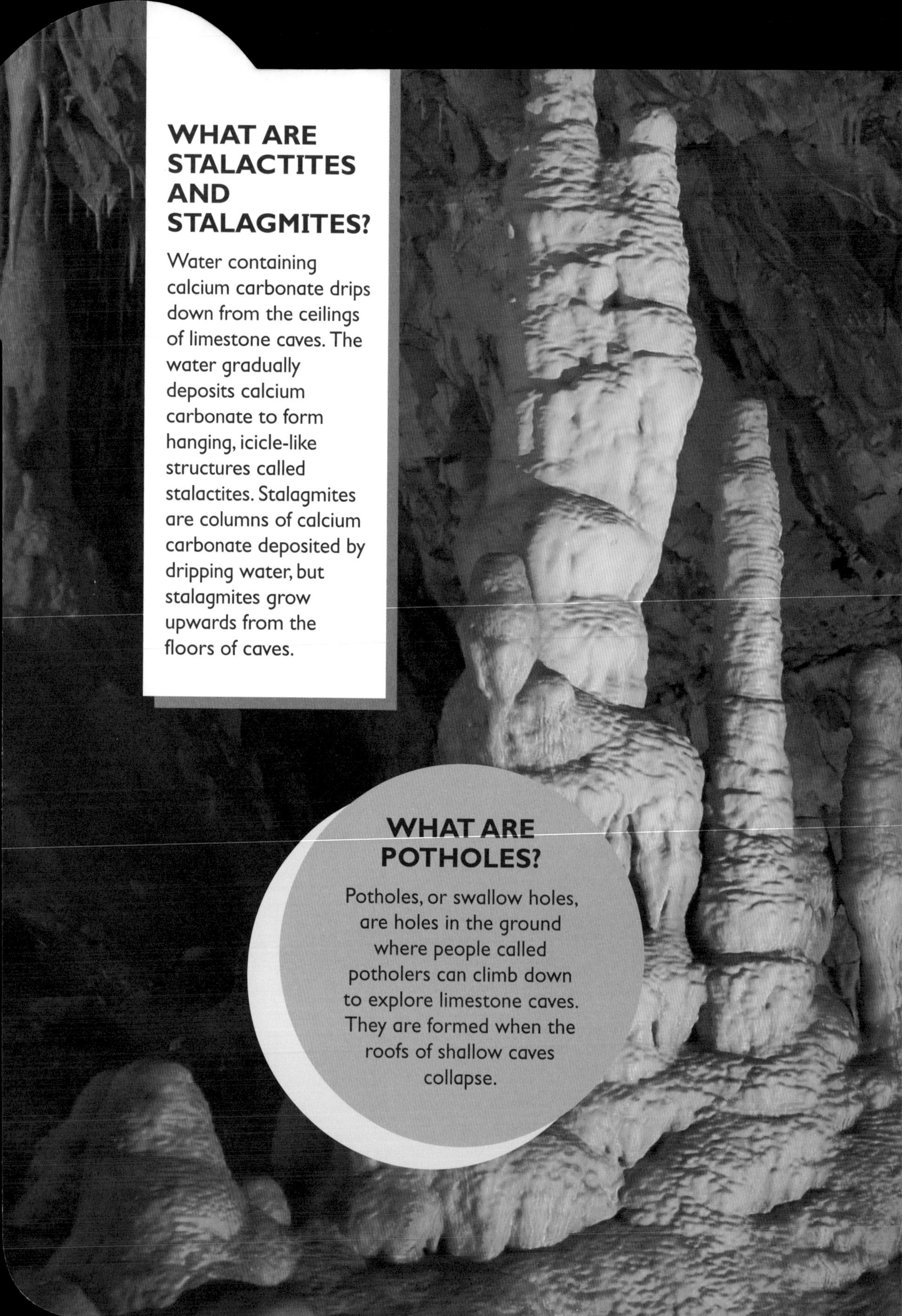

WHAT ARE STALACTITES AND STALAGMITES?

Water containing calcium carbonate drips down from the ceilings of limestone caves. The water gradually deposits calcium carbonate to form hanging, icicle-like structures called stalactites. Stalagmites are columns of calcium carbonate deposited by dripping water, but stalagmites grow upwards from the floors of caves.

WHAT ARE POTHOLES?

Potholes, or swallow holes, are holes in the ground where people called potholers can climb down to explore limestone caves. They are formed when the roofs of shallow caves collapse.

WHAT IS GROUND WATER?

Ground water is water that seeps slowly through rocks, such as sandstones and limestones. The top level of the water in the rocks is called the water table. Wells are dug down to the water table.

WHY DO WATERFALLS OCCUR?

Waterfalls can occur when rivers cross hard rocks. When softer rocks downstream are worn away, the hard rocks form a ledge over which the river plunges in a waterfall.

WHERE DO RIVERS START?

Some rivers start at springs, where ground water reaches the surface. Others start at the ends of melting glaciers or are the outlets of lakes.

HOW DO RIVERS WEAR AWAY THE LAND?

Young rivers push loose rocks down steep slopes. The rocks rub against riverbeds and deepen valleys. The rocks also rub against each other and break into finer pieces.

HOW DO CANYONS FORM?

A fast-moving river carrying large rocks can slowly wear away the riverbed. Over time, the river may erode a steep canyon.

WHAT IS AN OXBOW LAKE?

Sometimes slow-flowing rivers change course. Cut-off bends become oxbow lakes, with a distinctive curved shape.

WHAT ARE DELTAS?

Deltas are areas of sediments, made up of sand, mud and silt, that pile up around the mouths of some rivers.

WHAT ARE TRIBUTARY RIVERS?

Tributary rivers are rivers that flow into a main river.

HOW DOES WATER WEATHER ROCKS?

Water dissolves rock salt. It also reacts with some types of the hard rock granite, turning minerals in the rock into a clay called kaolin.

WHAT ARE ARCHES AND STACKS?

Waves hollow out arches in rocky headlands, which eventually collapse into stacks.

HOW CAN PEOPLE SLOW DOWN WAVE EROSION?

On many beaches, structures are built at right angles to the shore. These groynes slow down the movement of sand by waves and currents.

WHAT IS A BLOWHOLE?

It is a hole in the rock above a sea cave. When waves enter the cave's mouth, they travel up into the blowhole, sometimes causing blasts of water.

WHAT IS A BAYMOUTH BAR?

Some spits join one headland to another. They are called baymouth bars, because they can cut off bays from the sea, turning them into enclosed lagoons.

WHAT ARE SPITS?

In places where the coasts change direction, sand and pebbles pile up in narrow ridges called spits.

DOES THE SEA WEAR AWAY THE LAND?

Waves wear away soft rocks to form bays, while harder rocks on either side form headlands.

HOW QUICKLY IS THE LAND WORN AWAY?

An average of 3.5 centimetres is worn away in 100 years. Over millions of years, mountains can be worn down to plains.

WHAT IS A GLACIER?

A glacier is a slow-moving river of ice. Glaciers form in cold mountain areas, when snow compacts into ice. Eventually, the ice starts to move downhill. Rocks frozen into the glaciers erode the valleys through which they flow.

WHICH IS THE LARGEST GLACIER?

The Lambert Glacier in Antarctica is the world's largest. It is 500 kilometres long.

IS GLOBAL WARMING MAKING THE GLACIERS MELT?

Rising temperatures are making glaciers shrink and disappear all over the world. Some glaciers are retreating at a rate of 15 metres every year.

WHAT IS A GLACIAL LAKE?

A melting glacier often leaves behind large patches of ice in hollows along its path. These will eventually melt to create lakes.

HOW CAN WE TELL THAT AN AREA WAS ONCE COVERED BY ICE?

Mountain areas contain steep-sided valleys worn by glaciers. Armchair-shaped basins where glacier ice formed are called cirques.

WHAT HAPPENS IN AN ICE AGE?

During ice ages, temperatures fall and ice sheets spread over large areas. Several ice ages have occurred in Earth's history, dramatically shaping our planet.

WHAT ARE THE WORLD'S LARGEST BODIES OF ICE?

Today, the largest bodies of ice are the ice sheets of Antarctica and Greenland.

WHAT ARE FJORDS?

Fjords are deep, water-filled valleys that wind inland along coasts. They were once river valleys that were deepened by glaciers during the last ice age.

WHEN WAS THE LAST ICE AGE?

The last ice age began about 1.6 million years ago and ended 10,000 years ago.

HOW MUCH OF THE WORLD IS COVERED BY ICE?

Ice covers about 10% of the world's land.

WHERE ARE THE POLES?

The North Pole lies in the middle of the Arctic Ocean, which is covered by sea ice for much of the year. The South Pole lies in the freezing continent of Antarctica, which is covered by the world's largest ice sheet.

IS THE POLAR ICE MELTING?

Yes. Climate change is raising global temperatures, which is affecting the polar ice sheets and sea ice. By 2040, the Arctic Ocean may be free from sea ice in the summer.

HOW MUCH ICE IS IN ANTARCTICA?

Ice and snow cover 98% of Antarctica. The Antarctic ice sheet is the world's largest and contains about seven-tenths of the world's fresh water.

IS ANTARCTICA'S ICE SHEET GETTING THINNER?

Yes. In West Antarctica, rising temperatures are thinning the ice by about 1 metre per year.

WHY ARE ICEBERGS DANGEROUS?

Icebergs are huge chunks of ice that naturally break off from glaciers. They float in the sea with nine-tenths of their bulk submerged, which makes them very dangerous to ships.

HOW THICK IS THE ICE IN ANTARCTICA?

In places, the ice is up to 4.8 kilometres thick.

WHAT ARE ICE SHELVES?

Ice shelves are large blocks of ice joined to Antarctica's ice sheet, but which jut out over the sea.

HOW ARE THE DESERTS CHANGING?

In deserts, wind-blown sand is important in shaping the scenery. It acts like the sand-blasters used to clean dirty city buildings. It polishes rocks, hollows out caves in cliffs and shapes boulders.

HOW ARE SAND DUNES FORMED?

The wind blowing across a desert piles the sand up in hills called dunes.

CAN WATER CHANGE DESERT SCENERY?

Thousands of years ago, many deserts were rainy areas and many land features were shaped by rivers. Flash floods sometimes occur in deserts. They sweep away much worn material.

ARE ALL DESERTS SANDY?

Only about 20% of all desert land is sandy. Nearly all hot deserts are plains where the wind has exposed rock, gravel or sand.

WHAT IS A MUSHROOM ROCK?

It is a top-heavy, mushroom-shaped boulder whose base has been worn away by wind-blown sand.

WHAT ARE DUST STORMS?

During dust storms, desert winds sweep fine dust high into the air.

WHAT IS A WADI?

Wadis are dry waterways in deserts.

WHAT ARE BARCHANS?

Barchans are crescent-shaped dunes in the desert. They form when winds blow mainly from one direction.

WHAT IS DEFORESTATION?

When trees are cut down without new trees being planted, deforestation takes place. Today, the tropical rainforests are particularly affected by deforestation. These forests contain more than half of the world's species – many are threatened with extinction.

WHAT IS GLOBAL WARMING?

It is a rise in average worldwide temperatures. This is partly caused by activities such as deforestation and the burning of fossil fuels, such as coal. These activities release greenhouse gases, such as the carbon dioxide stored in trees. These gases trap heat in the Earth's atmosphere. Global warming is likely to cause changes in rainfall patterns, causing floods in some areas and droughts in others.

WHAT IS AIR POLLUTION?

Air pollution occurs when gases such as carbon dioxide are emitted into the air by factories, homes and offices. Vehicles also cause air pollution, which produces city smogs, acid rain and global warming.

WHAT IS SOIL EROSION?

Soil erosion occurs when people cut down trees and farm the land. Soil erosion on land made bare by people is a much faster process than natural erosion.

HOW MUCH FOREST IS CUT DOWN EACH YEAR?

Around 13 million hectares of forest are lost each year.

WHAT IS DESERTIFICATION?

Desertification is when fertile land is turned into desert. This is caused by cutting down trees, overgrazing grassland, or by natural climate changes.

WILL GLOBAL WARMING AFFECT ANY ISLAND NATIONS?

If global warming melts the world's ice, then sea levels will rise. Low-lying countries such as the Maldives and Kiribati could vanish under the waves.

WHAT IS A DAM?

A dam is a man-made barrier that holds back flowing water. Dams are often built to retain water in order to generate hydroelectric power or for irrigation.

CAN DESERTS BE FARMED?

Yes. In the USA and other countries, barren deserts are watered from wells that tap ground water, or water piped from faraway areas.

HOW HAVE PEOPLE TURNED SEA INTO LAND?

The Dutch have created new land by building dykes called polders around areas once under the sea. Rainwater washes the salt from the soil and the polder land finally becomes fertile.

CAN THE POLLUTION OF RIVERS HARM PEOPLE?

When factories pump poisonous wastes into rivers, creatures living near the rivers' mouths, such as shellfish, absorb the poison. When people eat such creatures, they, too, are poisoned.

WHAT IS THREATENING FISH IN THE SEA?

Coral reefs and mangrove swamps are breeding places for many fishes. The destruction or pollution of these areas is threatening the numbers of fish in the oceans.

WHAT POLLUTES RIVERS?

Pollution in rivers includes rubbish, chemicals and sewage.

HOW ARE NATURAL WONDERS MADE?

Many of the Earth's beautiful features were created by weathering, erosion and the work of rivers, sea and ice.

WHERE IS...

...THE LONGEST BEACH?	Cox's Bazar Beach in Bangladesh is the longest sandy sea beach at 125 kilometres.
... THE LARGEST CANYON?	The Grand Canyon in the United States. It is 446 kilometres long and 1.6 kilometres deep.
... THE TALLEST STALAGMITE?	It may be in the cave of San Martin Infierno in Cuba, measuring 67.2 metres.
...THE GREAT PEBBLE?	Ayers Rock in central Australia is also known as 'Uluru', meaning 'great pebble'.
...THE GREAT BARRIER REEF?	It lies off the northeast coast of Australia and is about 2,000 kilometres long.
... 'SMOKE THAT THUNDERS'?	This is the local name of the beautiful Victoria Falls on the Zambezi River in Africa.

WHERE ARE THE NEEDLES?

The Needles are a row of chalk stacks, eroded by waves, that lie off the Isle of Wight in southern England.

WHAT ARE HOODOOS?

Hoodoos can be seen at Bryce Canyon in the United States. These rock needles are formed by water, wind and ice erosion.

WHERE IS THE MATTERHORN?

The Matterhorn is a magnificent mountain on Switzerland's border with Italy.

HOW TALL IS THE MATTERHORN?

The Matterhorn reaches a height of 4,478 metres above sea level.

WHAT IS THE GREAT BARRIER REEF? It is the world's longest group of coral reefs and islands.

IS THERE A LAKE UNDER ANTARCTICA? Yes. Scientists have found a lake, about the size of Lake Ontario in North America, hidden under Antarctica.

HOW ARE NATURAL WONDERS PROTECTED? In 1872, the world's first national park was founded at Yellowstone in the northwestern United States. Since then, national parks have been founded around the world to protect natural wonders.

WHICH JAPANESE WONDER ATTRACTS PILGRIMS? Mount Fuji in Japan is regarded as a sacred mountain by many people, who make long pilgrimages to the top.

HOW MANY...

MUSCLES ARE IN THE HUMAN BODY?

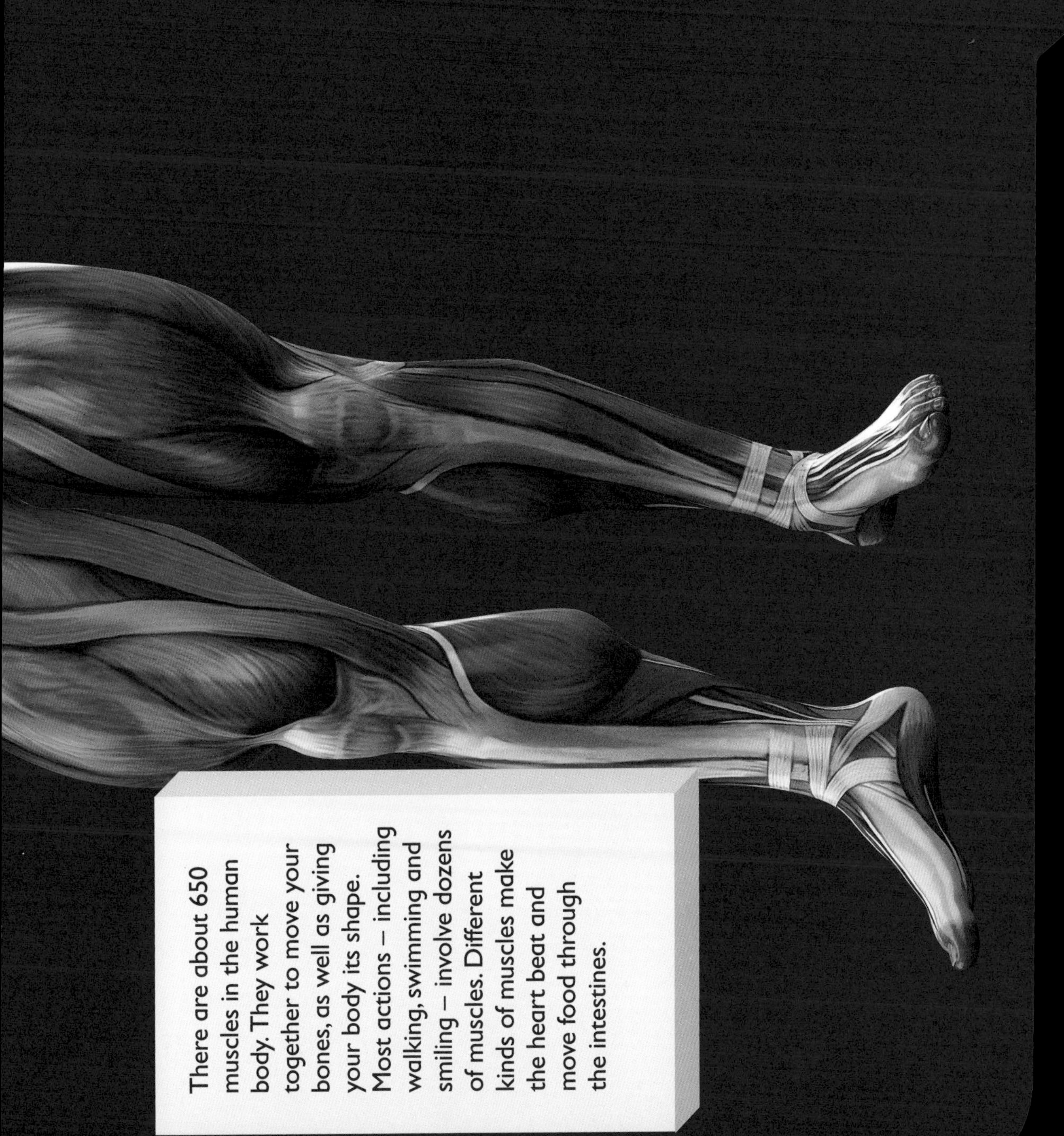

There are about 650 muscles in the human body. They work together to move your bones, as well as giving your body its shape. Most actions – including walking, swimming and smiling – involve dozens of muscles. Different kinds of muscles make the heart beat and move food through the intestines.

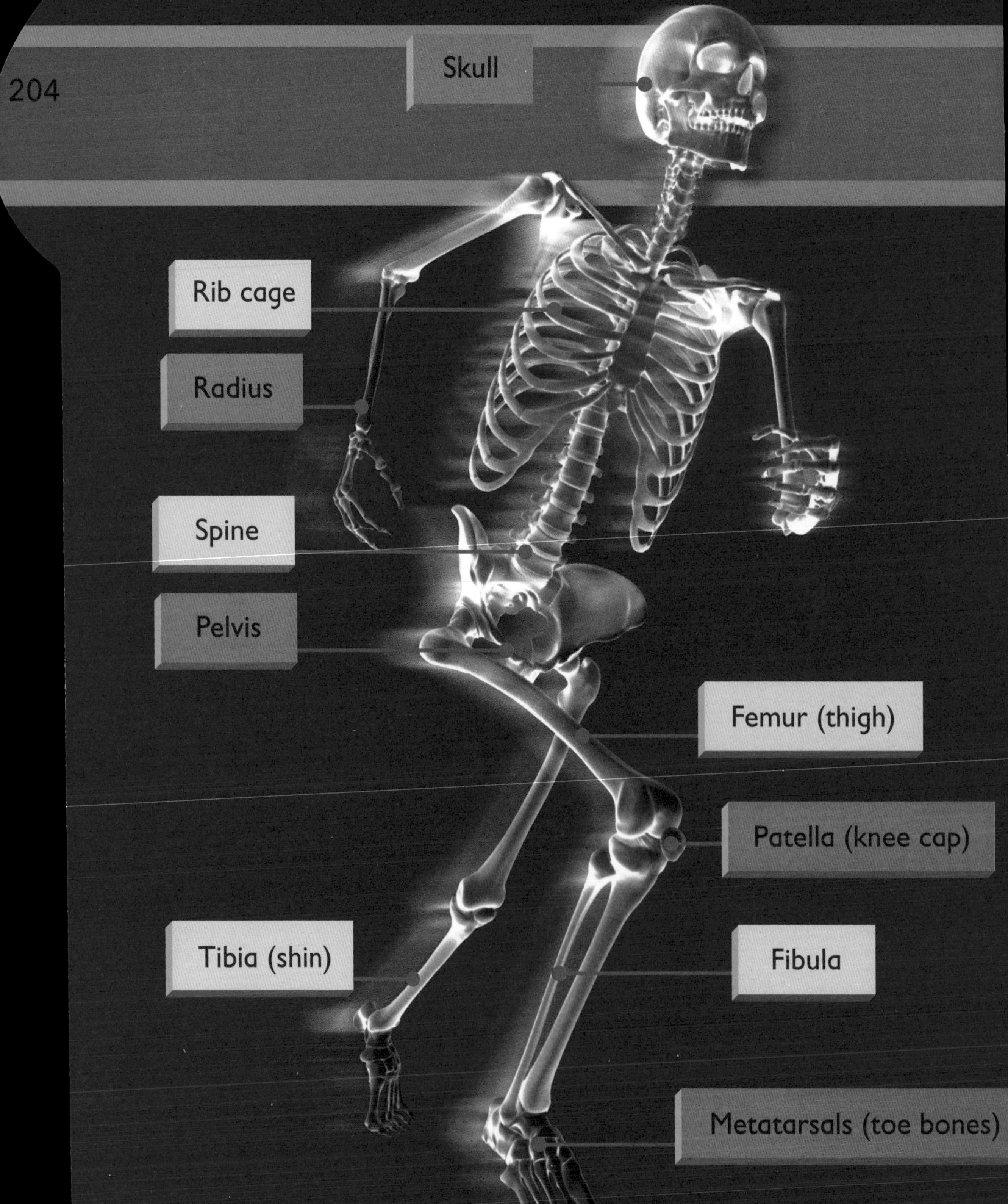
Skull
Rib cage
Radius
Spine
Pelvis
Femur (thigh)
Patella (knee cap)
Tibia (shin)
Fibula
Metatarsals (toe bones)

WHAT DOES THE SKULL DO?

The skull is a hard covering of bone that protects the brain like a helmet. All the bones of the skull except the lower jaw are fused together to make them stronger.

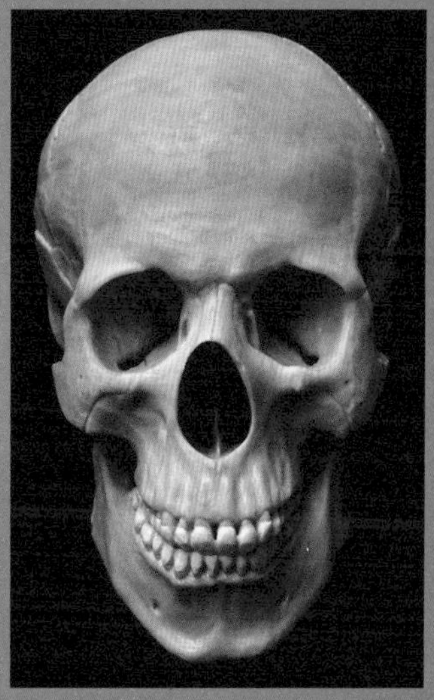

HOW MANY VERTEBRAE ARE THERE IN THE SPINE?

A vertebra is a knobbly bone in your spine. The 33 vertebrae fit together to make a strong pillar, the spine, which carries much of your weight.

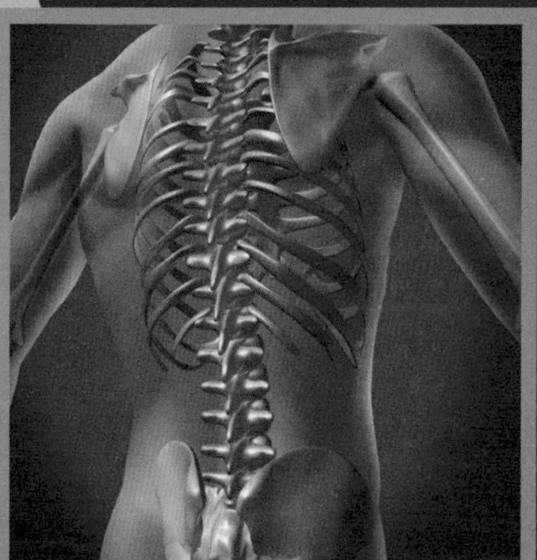

WHICH IS THE LONGEST BONE?

The thigh bone, or femur, in the upper part of the leg is the longest bone in the body. It accounts for more than a quarter of an adult's height.

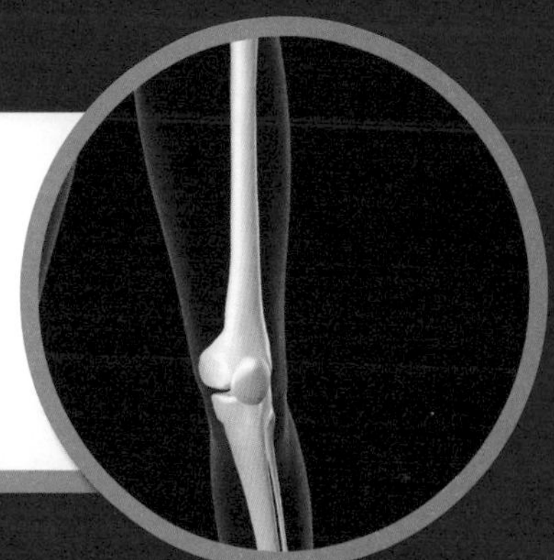

WHAT DOES SKIN DO?

Skin stops the moisture inside the body from getting out and stops germs getting in. Tiny particles in the skin also help to shield your body from the Sun's harmful rays.

WHAT IS A FINGERPRINT?

A fingerprint is made by thin ridges of skin on the tip of each finger and thumb. The ridges form a pattern of lines, loops or whorls.

ARE FINGERPRINTS UNIQUE?

Yes! Every person's fingerprint is different. Fingerprints are often used for identification.

WHY DO WE HAVE NAILS?

Nails protect our fingers and toes as well as helping us to grasp objects.

HOW FAST DO NAILS GROW?

A fingernail grows about 1 millimetre every 7 days.

WHY DOES HAIR FALL OUT?

No hair lasts more than about six years. Every day you lose about 60 hairs.

WHY DOES SKIN HAVE PORES?

Skin has tiny holes, called pores, to let out sweat when you are too hot.

WHAT GIVES HAIR ITS COLOUR?

Hair colour depends on a pigment called melanin. Lighter melanin causes blond or red hair. Darker melanin causes brown or black hair.

HOW FAST DO NERVES ACT?

A nerve signal travels at about 1 metre per second in the slowest nerves to more than 100 metres per second in the fastest.

HOW DOES A NERVE WORK?

A chain of nerve cells carries a signal to or from the brain. The electrical impulse is received by the nerve endings and sent from one nerve cell to the next.

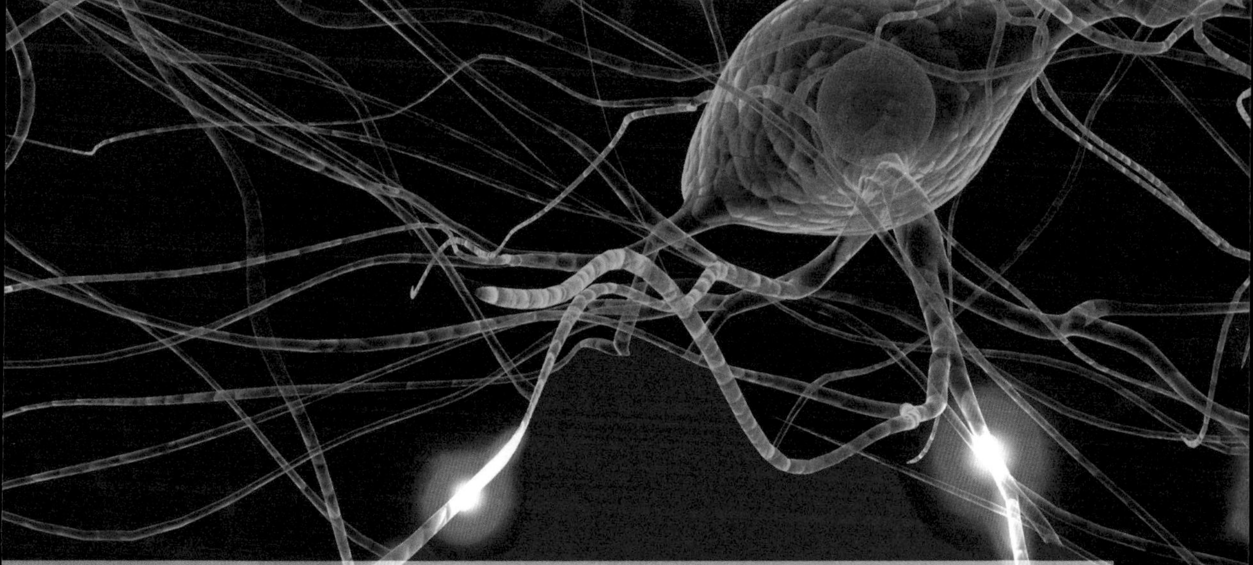

WHAT ARE THE BODY'S FIVE MAIN SENSES?

The five main senses are seeing, hearing, smelling, tasting and touching.

HOW DOES TOUCH WORK?

Different kinds of sense receptors in the skin react to touch, heat, cold and pain. The brain puts together all the different messages to tell you if something is shiny, wet, cold and many other things.

CAN BLIND PEOPLE USE TOUCH TO READ?

Yes. Blind people can run their fingertips over Braille – a pattern of raised dots that represent different letters.

HOW DOES SMELL WORK?

A smell is made by tiny particles in the air. When you breathe in, these particles dissolve in mucus in the nose. Smell receptors in the nose respond to this and send a message to the brain.

HOW DO YOU DETECT TASTE?

As you chew, tiny particles of food dissolve in saliva and trickle down to the taste buds on the tongue. The taste receptors react and send messages to the brain.

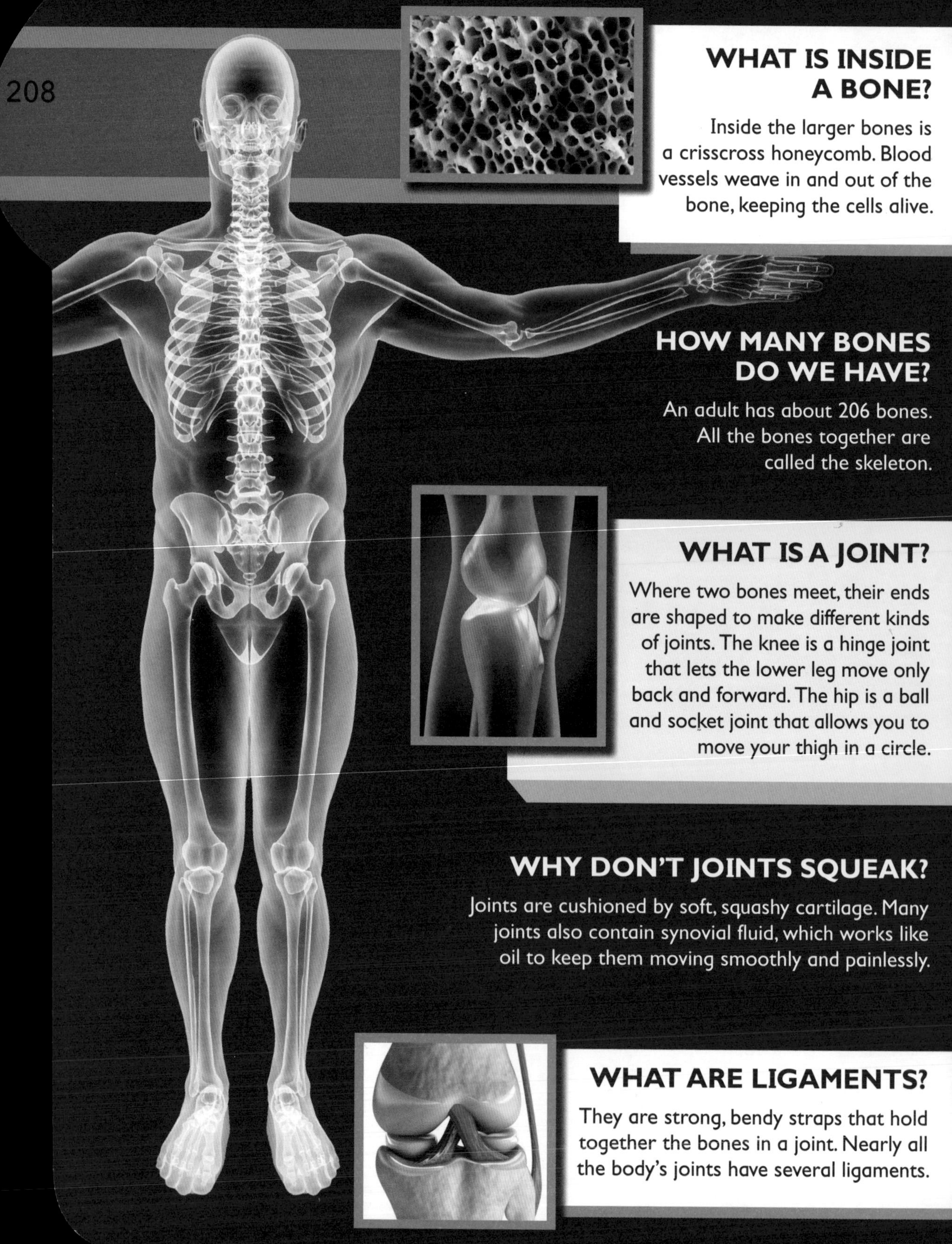

WHAT IS INSIDE A BONE?

Inside the larger bones is a crisscross honeycomb. Blood vessels weave in and out of the bone, keeping the cells alive.

HOW MANY BONES DO WE HAVE?

An adult has about 206 bones. All the bones together are called the skeleton.

WHAT IS A JOINT?

Where two bones meet, their ends are shaped to make different kinds of joints. The knee is a hinge joint that lets the lower leg move only back and forward. The hip is a ball and socket joint that allows you to move your thigh in a circle.

WHY DON'T JOINTS SQUEAK?

Joints are cushioned by soft, squashy cartilage. Many joints also contain synovial fluid, which works like oil to keep them moving smoothly and painlessly.

WHAT ARE LIGAMENTS?

They are strong, bendy straps that hold together the bones in a joint. Nearly all the body's joints have several ligaments.

HOW DO MUSCLES WORK?

Muscles work by contracting. Each muscle is connected to at least two bones. When they contract, muscles get shorter and thicker, so they pull the bones together, causing the body to move.

WHICH IS THE BIGGEST MUSCLE?

The biggest muscle is the gluteus maximus in the buttock. You can use it to straighten your leg when you stand up and it makes a comfortable cushion to sit on.

WHY DO MUSCLES WORK IN PAIRS?

Because muscles cannot push, they can only pull. For example, to bend your elbow, you tighten the biceps muscle at the front of your upper arm. To straighten the elbow again, you relax the biceps and tighten the triceps muscle at the back of your upper arm.

WHY DOES EXERCISE MAKE MUSCLES STRONGER?

A muscle is made of bundles of fibres that contract when you use the muscle. The more you use the muscle, the thicker the fibres become.

WHAT IS A TENDON?

A tendon is like a rope that joins a muscle to a bone. If you bend and straighten your fingers, you can feel the tendons in the back of your hand.

WHAT HAPPENS WHEN YOU BREATHE?

When you breathe in, you pull air through the mouth or nose into the windpipe and down to the lungs. Oxygen in the air is passed into the blood, then carried to all parts of the body.

HOW DO YOU TALK?

When you breathe out, the air passes over the vocal cords in the voice box, or larynx, in the neck. When the cords vibrate, they make a sound. Changing the shape of your lips and tongue makes different sounds.

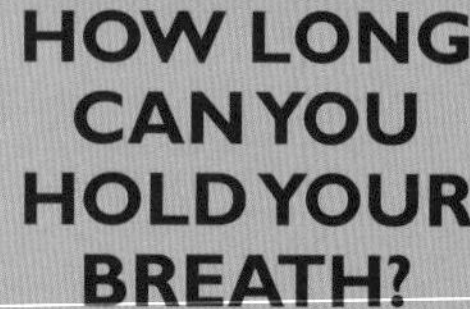

HOW LONG CAN YOU HOLD YOUR BREATH?

You can probably hold your breath for about a minute.

WHY...

... DO YOU COUGH?	To clear the air passages between your nose and lungs from mucus, dust or other particles.
... DOES RUNNING MAKE YOU PUFF?	Because your muscles are working hard and need extra oxygen.
... DO YOU SWEAT WHEN YOU ARE HOT?	To help cool the body. The salty liquid (sweat) takes heat from the body as it evaporates.
... IS BLOOD RED?	Blood gets its colour from billions of red blood cells, which contain haemoglobin.
... IS URINE YELLOW?	Because it contains traces of waste bile, which makes it yellowish.

WHAT DOES THE HEART DO?

The heart's job is to pump blood to the lungs and then all around the body. The right side of the heart pumps blood to the lungs. The left side takes blood filled with oxygen from the lungs and pumps it around the body.

WHAT DO WHITE BLOOD CELLS DO?

They surround and destroy germs and other intruders that get into the blood.

WHAT DOES THE LIVER DO?

The intestines pass digested food to the liver, where some nutrients may be released into the blood and the rest stored to be used later. The liver also processes poisons in the blood and changes unwanted proteins into urea.

WHAT IS...

... A CAPILLARY?	Blood travels through arteries, veins and smaller blood vessels. Capillaries are the tiniest of these.
... PLASMA?	It is a yellowish liquid in the blood, consisting of water with digested food and essential salts dissolved in it.
... URINE?	Urine is water combined with any unwanted substances that have been filtered from your kidneys.
... BILE?	Bile is a yellow-green liquid made by the liver. It helps to break up fatty food in the small intestine.

WHY ARE TEETH DIFFERENT SHAPES?

Different teeth do different jobs to help you chew up food. The broad, flat teeth at the front slice through food when you take a bite. They are called incisors. The pointed canine teeth grip and tear chewy food such as meat. The large premolars and molars grind the food between them into small pieces.

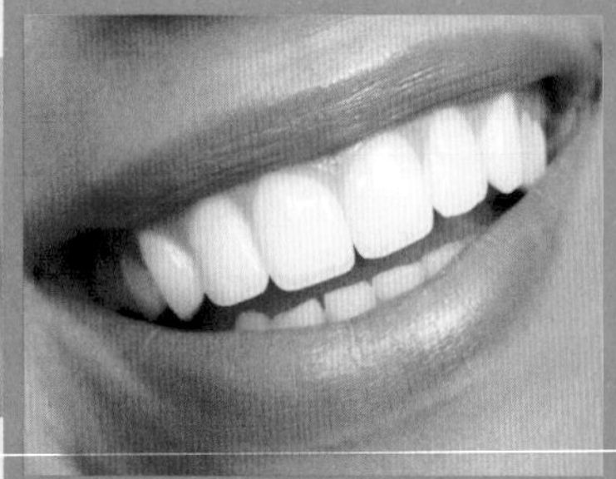

WHAT HAPPENS TO THE FOOD WE EAT?

After it is swallowed, food goes down the oesophagus into the stomach. Here it is broken down into a soupy liquid, before being squeezed through a coiled tube called the small intestine. The nourishing parts of the food are absorbed into the blood and the rest passes into the large intestine. About 24 hours after swallowing, the waste, called faeces, is pushed out of the body.

HOW LONG ARE THE INTESTINES?

The small intestine is more than three times as long as the whole body! In an adult this is about 6 metres. The large intestine is a further 1.5 metres and the whole tube from mouth to anus measures about 9 metres.

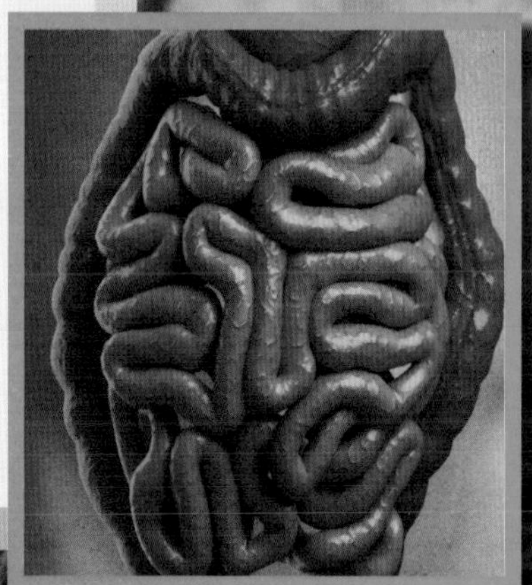

HOW DO YOU SEE SOMETHING?

You see an object when light bounces off it and enters your eyes. The black circle in the middle of the eye is called the pupil. Light passes through the pupil and is focused by the lens onto the retina at the back of the eye. The retina sends signals to the brain.

WHY DO YOU HAVE TWO EYES?

Two eyes help you to judge how far away something is. Each eye gets a slightly different picture, which the brain combines into a single 3D picture.

HOW BIG IS AN EYEBALL?

An adult eyeball is about the size of a golf ball, but most of the eyeball is hidden inside your head.

WHY DO YOU BLINK?

You blink to clean your eyes. Each eye is covered with a thin film of salty fluid, so every time you blink, the eyelid washes the eyeball.

WHY DOES THE PUPIL CHANGE SIZE?

The pupil becomes smaller in bright light to stop too much light from damaging the retina. In dim light the pupil opens to let in more light.

HOW DO YOU HEAR?

Sound reaches your ears as vibrations in the air. The vibrations travel to the eardrum, which makes the bones in the middle ear vibrate, too. These pass the vibrations to the fluid around the cochlea in the inner ear. Nerve endings in the cochlea send signals to the brain.

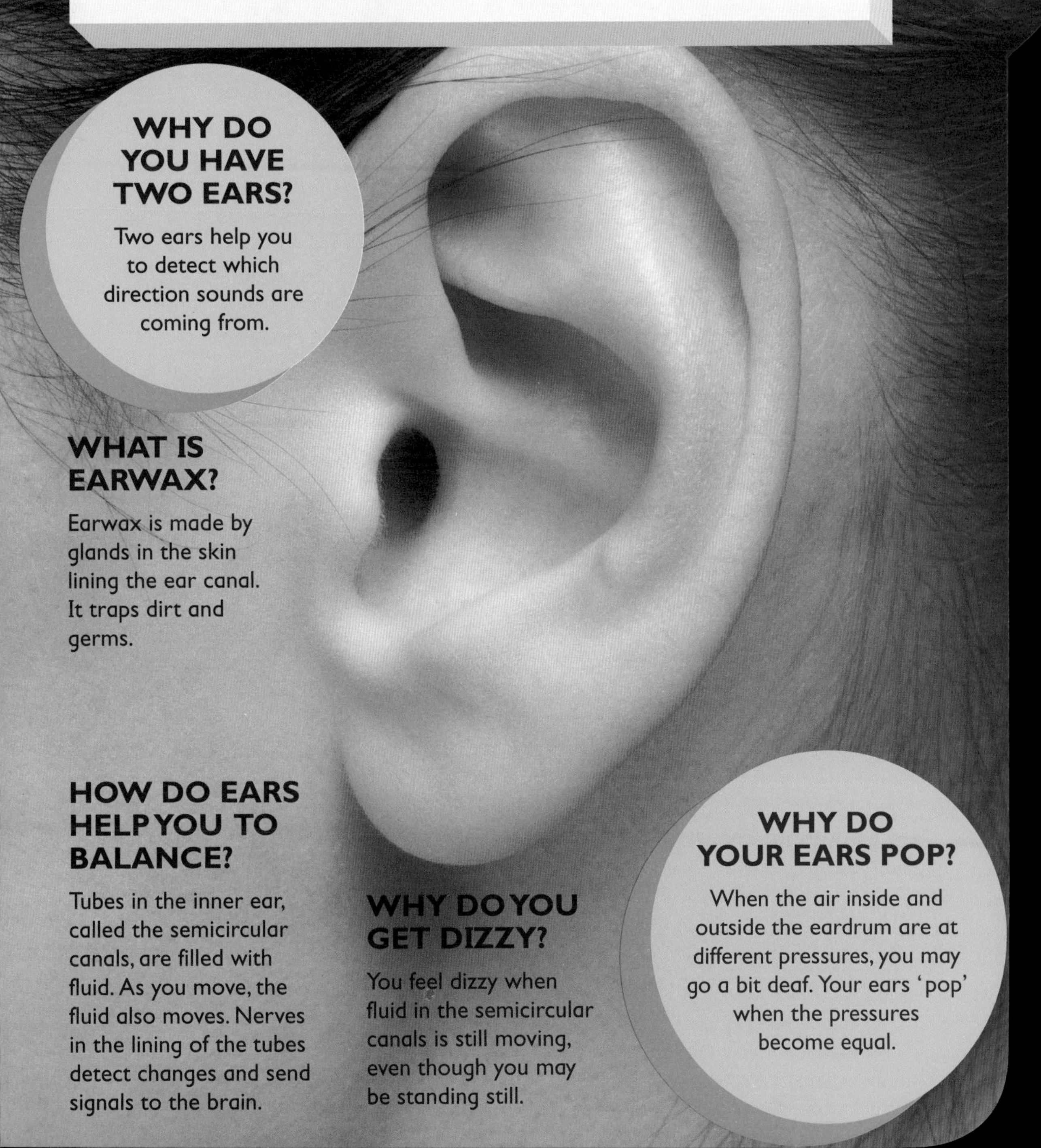

WHY DO YOU HAVE TWO EARS?

Two ears help you to detect which direction sounds are coming from.

WHAT IS EARWAX?

Earwax is made by glands in the skin lining the ear canal. It traps dirt and germs.

HOW DO EARS HELP YOU TO BALANCE?

Tubes in the inner ear, called the semicircular canals, are filled with fluid. As you move, the fluid also moves. Nerves in the lining of the tubes detect changes and send signals to the brain.

WHY DO YOU GET DIZZY?

You feel dizzy when fluid in the semicircular canals is still moving, even though you may be standing still.

WHY DO YOUR EARS POP?

When the air inside and outside the eardrum are at different pressures, you may go a bit deaf. Your ears ‘pop’ when the pressures become equal.

HOW ARE BABIES MADE?

A baby begins when a sperm from a man joins with an egg from a woman. The cells of the fertilized egg embed in the lining of the mother's womb, then multiply into an embryo.

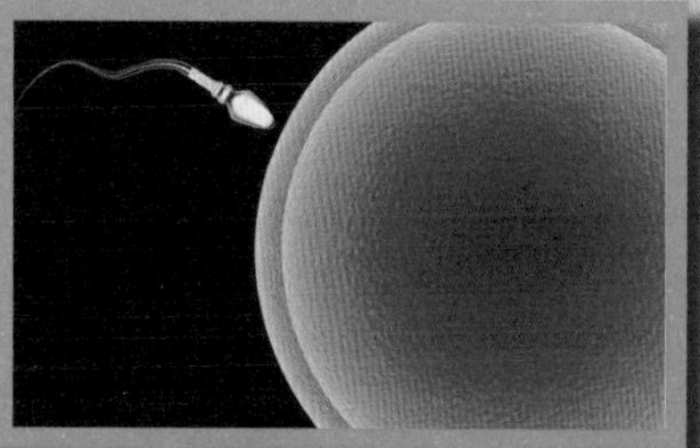

WHERE DOES A MAN'S SPERM COME FROM?

Sperm are made in a man's testicles, two sacs that hang to either side of his penis.

WHERE DOES THE EGG COME FROM?

A girl's eggs are stored in her two ovaries. After puberty, one of these eggs is released every month.

WHAT IS AN EMBRYO?

In the first seven weeks after conception, an unborn baby is called an embryo.

WHAT IS A FOETUS?

From eight weeks after conception until birth, an unborn baby is called a foetus.

WHEN DOES THE BABY HAVE A HEART?

Around eight weeks after conception almost every part of the baby has formed, including the heart.

HOW DOES AN UNBORN BABY FEED?

Most of the cells embedded in the womb grow into an organ called the placenta. Food and oxygen from the mother's blood pass through the placenta into the baby's blood.

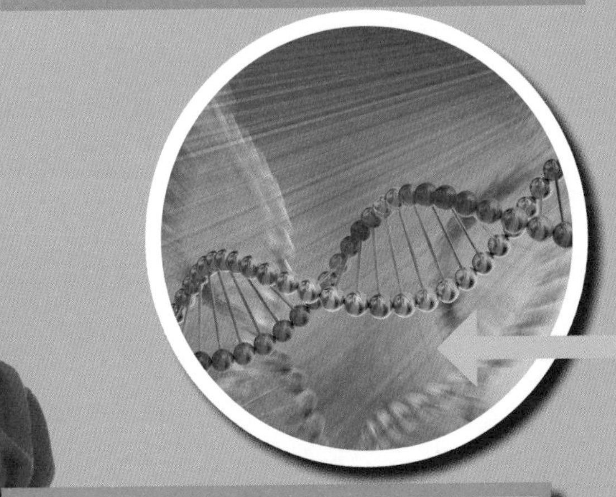

WHAT ARE GENES?

Genes are a combination of chemicals contained in each cell. They come from your mother and father and determine all your physical characteristics.

HOW FAST DOES AN UNBORN BABY GROW?

Three weeks after the egg is fertilized, the embryo is the size of a grain of rice. By the time it is born, the baby will probably be about 50 centimetres long.

HOW LONG DOES PREGNANCY LAST?

A baby usually grows in its mother's womb for 38 weeks.

WHAT HAPPENS WHEN A BABY IS BORN EARLY?

From about 24 weeks onwards, babies may survive in an incubator if they are born early.

HOW MUCH DOES A NEWBORN BABY WEIGH?

The average newborn weighs about 3.5 kilograms.

INDEX

ACKNOWLEDGEMENTS

t = top, b = bottom, l = left, r = right, m = middle

Cover images Shutterstock.com.
Images courtesy of Dreamstime.com, iStockphoto, Getty Images and Shutterstock.com.

Getty Images
42 Johnny Haglund/Getty Images, 88tr Hulton Archive/Getty Images, 88bl Hulton Archive/Getty Images, 61b Oliver Strewe/ Getty Images, 86-87b Panoramic Images/Getty Images, 107 Library of Congress - Oren Jack Turner/Getty Images, 156-157 J.A. Kraulis/Getty Images, 161m National Geographic/Getty Images.

Shutterstock.com
19tr Kletr/Shutterstock.com, 38b TonyV3112/Shutterstock.com, 55b PKOM/Shutterstock.com, 60bl Patricia Hofmeester/ Shutterstock.com, 81bl Ligados/Shutterstock.com, 99 Jason and Bonnie Grower/Shutterstock.com, 101b Natursports/Shutterstock.com, 106br Kharidehal Abhirama Ashwin/Shutterstock.com.